françois mauriac

The Christian Critic Series

fRancois mauRiac

Edited by
SISTER ANITA MARIE CASPARY, I.H.M.

Contributors
HENRI PEYRE
MICHAEL F. MOLONEY
SISTER ANITA MARIE CASPARY, I.H.M.
NEVILLE BRAYBROOKE
JAMES FINN

B. HERDER BOOK CO.
314 NORTH JEFFERSON
ST. LOUIS, MISSOURI 63103

The Christian Critic Series is under the general editorship of Harry J. Cargas, Director of the Foreign Student Program, Saint Louis University.

Library of Congress Catalog Card No. 68-26004

INTRODUCTION

The critic of Mauriac's fiction has today an opportunity perhaps unique in literary history. The unusual range and number of Mauriac's novels and the accompanying data provided by memoirs, journals and critical notes throughout a long and intensely productive life provide rich and complex materials for study. That the canon of Mauriac's novels may be closed is suggested by the author's statement in *Memoirs Interieurs* published in 1961, where he writes: "The aging novelist dreams the books which he no longer writes." [1]

For this reason, but even more because Mauriac's writing extends across a period representing widely varied literary styles and tastes, a re-examination of Mauriac's finest novels is presently valuable. From our immediate historical perspective, new meanings, and new statements at first not apparent, can now be observed within these novels. At the same time, those critical issues formerly thought of prime importance in the study of Mauriac have diminished in significance.

Mauriac's early novels met with a barrage of well-meaning but vituperative accusations especially from the pious and hypercritical Catholic critics of the twenties and thirties. For such novels as *The Desert of Love* and *Therese* he was condemned on the grounds of their frank treatment of brute lust and carnality.

While such an attack on Mauriac seems curiously outdated today, other typical Mauriac themes are seen as clearly prophetic of the self-criticism Catholicism is experiencing in the post Vatican II era. Among these are

Mauriac's condemnation of the selfishness and mediocrity of so-called Christian lives, hide-bound by tradition, impenetrable to the Gospel whose message they believe themselves to represent. Linked to this theme as illustration and commentary is Mauriac's picture of the bourgeois family, impregnable as social institution, but destructive of the life of the spirit. *Viper's Tangle* is perhaps the best of such portraits, with *Genetrix, The Frontenac Mystery, The Unknown Sea* and others.

Such judgments certainly are in accord with those of today's most advanced religious thinkers and writers. Yet even more surprising, as we re-study Mauriac, is the now apparent fact that much of his thought and insight corresponds to the work of existentialist philosophers. Both they and he search out the unauthentic, the complacent illusion, the fear of honest confrontation in human experience. They and he are obsessed with the isolation of the human person in an alien universe. Correlative is the disillusionment seemingly inevitable in human love. [2]

Seen in retrospect, however, the existentialist motif most evident in Mauriac's writing is the working-out of the search for self-knowledge and self-realization. Interestingly enough, this theme is most familiar to the contemporary reader from the writing of Gabriel Marcel, whose philosophic inquiries were being published almost contemporaneously with the novels of Mauriac. [3]

Whether Mauriac drew this particular intuition from Pascal, one of his "great men," and a common intellectual ancestor of both Marcel and Mauriac, or whether he was (less probably) affected by the existentialist philosophy developing in France and elsewhere throughout his own career is uncertain.

Certainly Mauriac is not a philosopher in the usual sense of that term, although the fictional mode is not alien to existentialist thinkers generally. What he says of himself, they would echo: "I am a metaphysician working in the concrete. . . . The sinner whom the theologian describes in the abstract, I clothe in flesh and blood." [4] Like existentialist philosophers, he explores with fidelity the psychological awareness of modern man, his isolation from his fellows, his search for self-identification, and his anxiety for a transcendent commitment.

For Mauriac, the world is indeed a somber place, but not for the reason that evil is an inherent and undefeated force therein. Rather does Mauriac center on the paradox rooted in man: the inviolable nature of his person as a unique human being with a destiny he alone can achieve and the inescapability of his fulfillment without surrender to Someone transcending himself. The sacredness of the human person is acknowledged first and recognized by the individual as he looks at himself in the light of the truth. As Canon Mouroux puts it, "man must learn to look himself in the face with perfect candour thanks to a deep-seated humility (often bitter enough), and to strive for self-mastery through an inexorable purification of his animal powers." [5]

Such self-recognition, such self-awareness comes slowly. It may be hindered by the network of relationships in which human beings find themselves. Dependencies upon others, social backgrounds with their perhaps atrophied customs and manners, even falsely conceived devotional life or exercises of piety may keep persons from a genuine and profound self-awareness. Sometimes a human being may become what others expect him to be; he may then fail to find and to actualize his authentic self. He may become so molded in the expectation of others that he is a faithful image of others' hopes and dreams, yet in that very act he loses his own identity.

A human being may be trapped in a social milieu or even enmeshed in a family tradition. He may fear the liberty which self-knowledge would bring. Sometimes he desires the security of conformity. And so meaningless lives are the lot of many, ironically even among so-called religious persons. These in a common predicament go from day to day in a dull round of duties and pleasures without ever having reflected deeply, self-deceived.

If self-recognition has been delayed or suppressed, it may be forced upon a man by anguish. As Father Dondeyne puts it: "When everything crumbles about him, when particular beings lose all meaning and value, man can awaken to himself and dispose himself to ask 'the fundamental question of philosophy' namely 'whether or not life is worth living.' " [6] In the solitude of such a moment, a human being may recognize himself for what he is—he begins to understand from the depths of suffering, failure, experience with death, his despair, that he is created by God and for God. From the depths of his being he may call for help on the only Being Who can assist him and he receives a response that renews life and hope. In the profundity of his consent to his relationship to God, a relationship of adoration, wonder and love, the person thus becomes free, understanding freedom as "the power we possess to realize ourselves in obedience to our own interior law, or better, to our constitutive call." [7] Since the end of the human person is union with God, he now realizes that liberty must "bring about . . . communion by an act that is both an act of obedience and an act of self-giving." [8]

Anguish of spirit and the visitations of misfortune or trouble, what the existentialist thinkers call "limit situations," [9] these are not desirable, certainly, in themselves. Yet these experiences are sometimes the only way in which insight into the mystery of existence may be gained. Such anguish is never the terminus, but rather the means by which the human person achieves a true relationship with God and fellow man.

This authentic act of self-knowledge and self-realization through the gift of self does not follow necessarily from membership in a Christian, a Catholic family. Nor do Christian education nor the background of a society at least nominally Christian make this engagement a *fait accompli*. St. Gregory of Nyssa writes: "Each of us is born by his own choice . . . and we are in some sort our own fathers because we bring ourselves to birth as we will." [10]

The baptized Christian, the regular church-goer, the contributor to charitable organizations may be blinded by complacency or false satisfaction to the reality of his relationship with God. It may be that only in the solitude of his inmost self, isolated by some sorrow or crisis, will such a "Christian" come to realize intensely that he is called to sonship of the Father by, through, and with his brother, the Incarnate Word.

Self-knowledge and the gift of self—it is in terms of these two existentialist themes that Mauriac writes the histories of human lives. It is true that he deals chiefly with man's failure or near-failure to acheve his true being. In the preface to *Trois Recits,* he wrote:

> And so I pride myself on painting a world in revolt against the Tribunal of conscience, a miserable world, devoid of Grace, and so, . . . to reach an indirect apology for Christianity. [11]

Certainly we find often in the novels of Mauriac shallow and complacent Christians carefully cushioning themselves from the shock of self-recognition. Sometimes we see them in another aspect—that of those who attest their self-knowledge, but who refuse the gift of themselves, serving only their ego, in a monstrous parody of life. It is on these individuals that Mauriac is especially harsh in judgment. [12]

Yet on the other hand we find those in his novels who are impelled by generosity to make the gift of self even before they know themselves for what they are, before they have opened themselves to God. Inevitably, as Mauriac reports, this spells tragedy for them. Is he then habitually pessimistic about human love as earlier critics have stated? Or is he rather insisting that the communion of real love cannot be achieved without the full acceptance of one's authentic self, and accordingly without corresponding knowledge of the unique dignity of the beloved?

Mauriac has shown us, too, others who make the gift of themselves not to a person, but in service of an abstract ideal such as justice, or truth, or beauty. Such individuals are portrayed as heroic types who fail pathetically to achieve fulfillment because their nature cries out for personal response from another, or from the Other.

Seldom does Mauriac choose to show us those who, recognizing themselves for what they are, give themselves fully to God in service, carrying on with Him a dialogue of love. Self-knowledge and self-realization here become reciprocal in growth. Mauriac usually portrays these rare persons as unattractive or misunderstood, perhaps to emphasize how little the approval of others is necessary for their peace or joy. Their common quality in Mauriac's work is a great-hearted generosity with which they freely offer their lives or their ambitions or their sufferings that others may live.

To read Mauriac against this background, only recently given us by existentialist philosophers, to read his novels in explication of this dual theme of self-knowledge and self-realization is to gain a new perspective which adds dimension to them as separate entities and which assembles all of Mauriac in a new unity.

SISTER ANITA MARIE CASPARY, I.H.M.
(Formerly known as Mother Mary Humiliata, I.H.M.)

NOTES

1 Francois Mauriac, *Memoirs Interieurs,* trans. Gerard Hopkins, Farrar, Straus & Cudahy, 1961, p. 239.

2 Michael F. Moloney, "The Metaphysic of Love," *Francois Mauriac, A Critical Study,* Alan Swallow, 1958, p. 75.

3 The parallel is dramatic when we recall that one of Mauriac's direct questions, "Why are you not one of us?" brought Marcel into the Roman Catholic Church.

4 *Journal* II.

5 Jean Mouroux, *The Meaning of Man,* trans. A. H. G. Downes, Sheed and Ward, 1948, p. 131, or Image Books (Doubleday Division) paperback, 1951.

6 Albert Dondeyne, *Contemporary European Thought and Christian Faith,* trans. Ernan McMullin and John Burnheim, Duquesne Studies Philosophical Series 8, pp. 90-91.

7 Mouroux, p. 147.

8 Mouroux, p. 147.

9 See Kurt F. Reinhardt, *The Existentialist Revolt,* Frederick Ungar Publishing Co., 1960, p. 236.

10 *Vita Moysis,* P. B. XLIV, 327 b.

11 Martin Jarrett-Kerr, C.R., *Francois Mauriac,* Bowes & Bowes, 1957, p. 35.

12 Pierre-Henri Simon, *Mauriac par lui-meme,* (Ecrivains De Toujours) Editions du Seuil, 1959, p. 60.

Contents

Henri Peyre

FRANCOIS MAURIAC

If the French critics of 1930-45 had been asked which
novelist, in their estimation, was the most likely to out-
live the wreckage of time and to rank next to Proust in
greatness, more votes would probably have been cast for
Mauriac than for any other living French writer, his rivals
being Malraux, Giono, and Bernanos, probably in that
order. Mauriac's eminence was comparatively unrecog-
nized in English-speaking countries, long after his elec-
tion to the French Academy in 1933 and even after the
Nobel Prize had been bestowed upon him. Translations
of his works have been coming out timidly. The utmost
tribute, that of a Pocket Books edition with a seductive
or a sickening cover (as tastes may go), came to the
Desert of Love only in 1953. The brevity of Mauriac's
récits may have appeared unorthodox to publishers who
like a novel to conform to the supposed demands of solid
readers who insist that they get their money's worth in
weight. The poetic finish of his style may have frightened
off translators. But the pessimism of Mauriac's novels and
their Roman Catholic view of sin and of love must have
proved the chief deterrent to Anglo-Saxon readers. Pessimism, to be sure, abounds in their own fiction, but it dons
youthful violence, and evil is somehow depicted in glaring and alluring colors.

There were signs of a change in the tastes of many educated readers, at the very time (since 1945 or thereabout) when the compatriots of Mauriac tended to dismiss him as a classical writer who, afraid of spoiling his earlier successes through imitating himself, was driven to dramas and to journalism. Many students in American colleges were fascinated by Mauriac as a craftsman and also by the use he has made of the religious theme. Religion once again has become fashionable in fiction. It has been found by reassured critics to permeate James Joyce's work, to explain William Faulkner's portrayal of an evil that was original and hence ennobling, and to give a Catholic hue to Eugene O'Neill's plays and James T. Farrell's saga. The adjective 'Catholic' paired with the word 'novelist,' has, in the eyes of some readers, enhanced the stature of Graham Greene and Evelyn Waugh. Somerset Maugham made skillful use of the theme in *The Razor's Edge,* and Aldous Huxley wrote fondly of Machiavellian mystics like Father Joseph. But Mauriac's place in contemporary letters owes little to sectarianism or to tides of changing taste. Out of the score of novels he has published, four or five seem clearly destined for survival. Few are the novelists in any language of whom such a prophecy could be ventured.

If the factors at work at any one time in life and in art may be grouped into the conflicting forces of tradition and of experiment, Mauriac seems to rank with those novelists who have shunned the loudly advertised paths of experimentation. At a time when the *roman-fleuve* appeared as the order of the day and when juggling with the old-fashioned structural unity and with the continuous flow of time had become the first gesture of a writer asserting his modernity, Mauriac chose to compose isolated novels, strictly organized, with few of those contradictions and violent plunges into the unconscious that other Frenchmen took as evidence that they lived in a post-

Dostoevskian era. Once or twice, the same characters recur in two different books. But their creator had enough humility not to presume that his readers might, after several years, remember the earlier doings of certain women of ill repute or of angelic adolescents. He rightly feared the lack of freshness and the artificiality of novelists who have chained themselves, volume after volume, to the drawn-out career of a Forsyte or of a Jean-Christophe. Every one of Mauriac's novels is a fresh attempt and an adventure into the unknown, though every one of them ends monotonously with the gift of grace that the novelist insists upon imparting to his sinners.

Mauriac's fiction has been charged with monotony. It moves in a world that indeed is, geographically and socially, narrowly limited. It revolves around the same perennial obsessions with money, property, the enticements of the flesh, and the wages of sin. Within these confines, however, it explores in depth. What is more, it conjures up that diseased and haunted world, and gains in vivid intensity what is sacrificed in diversity. In contrast with several experimenters among contemporary novelists, Mauriac stands as the upholder of the traditional virtues of the French novel. He is fully aware of the new complexity that Stendhal, Dostoevski, and Proust have led us to expect from fiction. But his purpose is not to experiment with new fictional forms or to explore recesses of the unconscious with awe, or with the naiveté of one who has lately discovered the jargon of clinical psychology. He writes because he must rid himself of the obsession of his characters and endow with shapes and sounds the desolate world that he carries within his imagination. The traditional form of the French novel, condensed, linear in its development, and strongly tempted to return to the unities of the classical tragedy, suited his talent as it did the themes he treated. Like Racine's plays, his novels are dramatic presentations of a psychological crisis. The plot permits very few incidents, and only those that help bring out new aspects of the characters. His novels move swiftly to a relentless denouement. Indeed, their tension is so feverish that they could hardly last longer without becoming painful to the reader. They are no more relieved by humor, by the restful oasis of pure description or of lyrical escape than is Racinian tragedy. Within the traditional mold of the French novel, classical in its economy, swift in its pace, written with elaborate care for stylistic values, Mauriac subtly cast the molten lead of dark motives and destructive passions, such as we have come to expect from modern fiction since Balzac, Melville, and the great Russians.

Mauriac's date of birth, 1885, makes him one of the group of gifted French novelists who were to reach full manhood on the eve of World War I and to stage, in the years 1910-13, a literary renaissance in Paris. Martin du Gard, Giraudoux, Duhamel, Romains, Maurois, Alain-Fournier, Jouhandeau, and Bernanos belong to the same age group. Their ascendancy over French letters reached its height in 1925-35, when, with the exception of Alain-Fournier, who was killed in the war, they were to meet with an audience attuned to their music, and to produce their most accomplished work. Most of them belonged to the middle or lower strata of the bourgeoisie, whose creative vitality has remained astounding in France, despite savage attacks repeatedly launched against it by its own scions, from Flaubert to Mauriac himself. Most of them were provincials; and Mauriac's fiction, even after he had taken up residence in Paris, fed on the observations and memories accumulated in his provincial childhood.

The section of France to which he belongs with all his being had already given birth to many men of letters, most of them of a cheerful and humorous disposition, inclined to skeptical enjoyment of the varieties and inconsistencies of mankind. But Mauriac has little in common with Montaigne or Montesquieu, even with elusive Fénelon or with Rivière, also born in Bordeaux, in 1886, who searched for faith with the secret fear of being imprisoned in it if he once found it. The power of literature is such that the Bordeaux region and its inhabitants will henceforth appear to many in the gloomy hues lent to them by Mauriac's fiction, as Georgia and Mississippi have been stamped as lands of oppressive tragedy by contemporary American novelists. The traditional Gascon, with his bravado or with the playful irony that Renan thought he owed to his Gascon mother, the smiling beauty of his vineyards, and his Epicurean delight in choice food, never appear in Mauriac's stories of frustration and of remorse.

Yet Mauriac loves his native city of Bordeaux, its wine merchants and its lawyers, its *cafés* and its public gardens, where his characters repair, pleasure bound, when they leave their country estates to celebrate a rich crop or an advantageous sale of timber. Rather, he hates Bordeaux because he loves it too much, as he confessed at the end of his fragment of an autobiography, *Commencements d'une vie*. 'We hate our city as we do the being whom we love, for all that is usurped by that being, for the limits which it imposes upon us; it sets irreparable bounds upon our existence, and defrauds us of a higher fate.' His debt to his provincial childhood has been loudly and repeatedly proclaimed.

In fact, he confessed his inability to place any of his novels in a setting other than the one in which he grew; he compared the fascination thus wrought over him by his province to the blinding of a mule doomed to grind corn in its circular prison. When his characters rush to Paris, eager to escape for a brief respite from the passions that hold them captive in their drab familiar surroundings, they appear suddenly less real. The dance halls or the *cafés,* where they attempt to drown their regret for their childhood and for their native village, are depicted as some

5

devil's den in a modern Babylon. The characters who had hoped to escape from themselves remain provincials in exile. 'The provinces are Pharisaic,' said Mauriac in a small book of notes and maxims on that subject, *La Province*. 'Only in the provinces do people know how to hate well. . . . The provinces condemn most women to chastity. [1] How many of them lacked the vocation for it. . . . Every writer leaving his province for Paris is a fugitive Emma Bovary.' But life is more intense because it is less subject to idle diversion than in Paris. The human heart can be more easily laid bare to one who, as a youth in his teens, had silently observed his elders, dreamed about women whom he would never approach, tamed his wild desires, and stifled his rebellious sobs.

The child, in Mauriac, is father of the man. He was molded by his early memories. Malagar, the country house in which he takes refuge every summer, has been repeatedly transfigured by him into a setting for his stories. Langon, which has become a gloomy abode of the dying wife and of the domineering mother-in-law in *Genitrix*, situated near the railway line between Bordeaux and Sète, was his grandfather's property. That grandfather, stubborn and anticlerical, who was converted on his dying day, has provided his grandson with a few features of the pathetic old man in *Le Noeud de vipères* (*Viper's Tangle*). Therésè's house, named Argelouse in the novel, was that of Mauriac's maternal grandmother. The rumbling, packed streetcar in which, every evening, young Courrèges first met Maria Cross, was familiar to Mauriac when he was completing his secondary school in Bordeaux. Mauriac's own father died when he was but eighteen months old. The child, along with three brothers and one sister, was brought up entirely by the young widow. The father had been an unbeliever, the mother was sternly religious, with a deep tinge of Jansenism to her Roman Catholic faith. The evening prayer, uttered by the mother with her five children around her under the crucifix, was a solemn rite.

Then the children would go to sleep, their arms crossed on their breasts, as demanded by God. They scrupulously observed the strictest rules, to the point of not eating the crust of their bread on Friday if it appeared slightly yellow, hence tainted with the yolk of eggs, thus infringing upon the observance of fasting. The fear of sin, first conceived as disobedience, haunted them; God was the formidable chastiser of the Old Testament rather than the merciful forgiver of the Gospels. Death was often present to them, as the dire event that might at any moment force them to appear before their Creator in a state of unreadiness.

Yet Mauriac's childhood was a happy one. He liked solitude and found it, even at school, where he seldom took part in games and sports. His faith was a source of deep inner joy to him. His meditative habits developed in him a precocious sensitiveness to nature. He feared the beauty of the fields and the hills, yet drank it avidly. Unlike the Psalmist, he could not read the glory of God's bounty in the starry nights and the fragrant orchards in springtime. 'Cybele has more worshippers in France than has Christ,' he wrote, denouncing the religion of the earth as the most potent religion among French peasants. He, too, was swayed by that pagan cult; the struggle between earthly and earthy attachments and a thirst for divine grace is an ever-recurring one in his characters. His early studies in a religious school near home developed religious sensibility in him and the other schoolboys but did little towards fostering religious intelligence, as he later remarked. Pascal was the favorite writer of the youth; although he later took him to task for his Jansenism, Mauriac remained his spiritual descendant. His fiction has aptly and skillfully been defined, by those who defended its orthodoxy against timid souls who smelled heresy in it, as the concrete expansion of a title suggested by Pascal for a whole section of his *Pensées*: 'Misery of the world without God.'

Mauriac completed his secondary studies at the *lycée* of Bordeaux. He passed his baccalaureate and went to Paris to pursue his scholarly education. Paleography and medieval archaeology then attracted him, and, after passing the required tests, he entered the *Ecole des Chartes,* where curators of French archives and medievalists are trained. However, he soon resigned from the *Ecole des Chartes.* His was not the scholar's patient and modest gift. He carried an ardent world within him, made up of memories of his province, of human desires and temptations, and, even more, of an impossible conflict between human and divine love. His ambition was to translate that inner universe into words.

Along with Pascal and Racine, who were, among the French classics, the chief builders of his soul, the writers he admired were the more sincere and the more tormented of the romantics. He admired Alfred de Vigny, whose thoughtful poetry attracted him in spite of, or perhaps because of, its passionate revolt against God, which Mauriac tended to prefer to conservative religious complacency. He felt close to Maurice de Guérin (1810-39), who worshipped nature with a burning fervor that set him apart from other French romantics. Guérin was a pagan and a pantheist tempted by Christ, struggling to be a true Christian but engulfed by the worship of the elements celebrated in his famous prose poem, *Le Centaure.* A centaur himself, he aspired toward the serenity of the heavens but was held back by animal life and earthly beauty. Jean Lacordaire and Félicité de Lamennais were also his spiritual and literary intercessors, the first for his eloquent charity and because 'he dares call human love by its name; the flesh and the blood are not silenced by him,' the second because he rejected the placid comfort of orthodoxy and a religion unmoved by the sufferings of the poor. Baudelaire's fame was spreading among the French youth in 1905-10, when Mauriac was himself courting the muse. One of his early essays vindicated *Les Fleurs du mal* against the Catholic critics who tried to reject such poetry on account of the poet's life or his occasional blasphemies. Mauriac, already, advanced the assertion that a sinner who half repenteth or who, like Baudelaire, with remorse and anguish damns himself is more truly Christian than many a virtuous man who has, like the philosopher Taine, led an impeccable life.

Among the writers then living, Mauriac, on the threshold of his literary career, was attracted by Barrès. At the age of sixteen, he drew comfort from a formula in *Un Homme libre,* one of Barrès's early novels, which described what the provincial adolescent was then practicing: 'to feel as much as possible while analyzing oneself as much as possible.' Mauriac rejoiced in his youthful sorrows, which made him a younger brother of those men of letters whose biographies he was devouring at that time. During his solitary years in Bordeaux and later among the temptations of the metropolis, the young Mauriac was followed by his familiar daemon, the daemon of self-knowledge (the title of his most searching short story was 'Le Démon de la connaissance'). Soon, however, he discovered, like all born novelists, that it is easier to know oneself by lending one's own feelings to imaginary creatures and developing them to the full than by remaining confined to complacent introspection. He cultivated in himself 'the fondness for taking a voluptuous interest in souls' that he attributed to one of the characters in his earliest novel.

Mauriac's literary debut, with two volumes of verse, was hailed by Barrès in 1909 and 1911. Soon after, the young poet, having married, gave up formal poetry, in which he felt his style was always cramped, and adopted the form of the novel. He returned to poetry only after his fiftieth year, in *Atys.* His early attempts at fiction, *L'Enfant chargé de chaines* (1913) and *La Robe prétexte*

(1914), are immature and overinclined to lyrical exuberance, which detracts from the convincingness that the plot and characters might have had. The author, already the father of a child, served in the army during World War I. The war, as a theme, left little trace in his work; but, in its gloomiest year, while a member of the expeditionary force on the Macedonian front in 1917, he meditated on the French moralists of whom he knew himself to be the heir. He strengthened his resolve to follow in their footsteps. But his ambition was to be a Christian moralist because he considered the Christian as the truest of all humanists since, 'to reach God, he must cross the whole of himself, and see the light dawn only through and beyond his own heart.' [2]

On his return to civilian life, Mauriac brought out two brief, ardent, but still unconvincing and youthful novels: *La Chair et le sang* (1920) and *Préséances* (1921). They, as well as a stronger work, *Le Fleuve de feu* (1923), are permeated with the obsession of the flesh. The delight of the senses is depicted as mysteriously entrancing, driving the characters to wild forsaking of all self-control and even to suicide. Yet those carnal pleasures are not merely the snares of the Devil. The power of love is great because we are aware of its frailty, we desperately try to embrace a beautiful body and to discover a soul behind it because we dread soon to be deprived of such ephemeral loveliness. Fear of the passing of time and of our own hasty march toward old age and death, search for self-oblivion in the abysses of passion, dim realization that the sufferings of love and the disgust of our sins draw us nearer to religion—such are the feelings lurking in the frantic adolescents depicted in Mauriac's early novels.

With *Le Baiser au lépreux* (1922), Mauriac composed his first masterpiece. Weaker novels were still to alternate with others of rare finish and power. *Destins* (1928),

Ce qui était perdu (1930), *Le Mystère Frontenac* (1933), *Le Mal* (1935), *Les Anges noirs* (1936), *Les Chemins de la mer* (1939) are considered definitely feeble products of the novelist's pen. Even *La Fin de la nuit* (1935), 'Insomnie,' and Thérèse chez le docteur,' two striking, long short stories included in *Plongées* (1938), and *La Pharisienne* (1941), while far from negligible, suffer from blemishes that impair their effectiveness as a whole. The best of Mauriac lies, for us, in the five works to which closer attention will be given in these pages.

Jean Péloueyre, the lamentable hero of *Le Baiser au lépreux,* is depicted with relentless lucidity by Mauriac. He is hideously ugly, tortured by shyness and the consciousness of his ridiculousness, afraid of girls; he resorts to religion and especially to confession as a refuge from his inferiority. He discovers one day a page of Nietzsche branding the inferior breed of 'slaves' as ready prey for Christian ethics and exalting the will to power in man. [3] He resolves to shake his gnawing timidity and to ask a young woman, from a poorer peasant family, to marry him. She cannot say no, for the Péloueyres are a well-to-do family, envied and respected in the district, and, as the priest explains to her, 'one does not refuse a Péloueyre.' Noémi, the husky peasant girl, like most of Mauriac's heroines, hardly looks for any physical pleasure in marriage; she will obey the law of religion and of her husband, and retain, through several pregnancies, a candid and almost virginal innocence. But the ugliness of Noémi's husband, the leper, whose soul, haunted by desire, becomes even more repulsive than his face, is too much even for her naïve good will. She embraces him, solely out of pity, and he, aware of the horror that he inspires, convinced that he never will be loved, flees to Paris for an impossible respite. He languishes away from her and from his familiar country surroundings, returns thin and pale, while she has involuntarily thrived in his absence.

11

He dies, mourned by his wife, to whom he has bequeathed his fortune on the condition that she shall not marry again. Repressing her buried youth and silencing the call of her flesh, she resigns herself to the eternal mourning clothes of the provincial widows and enters the only path open to her, that of self-denial.

In that brief, inhumanly hard novel, all the greatness of Mauriac's art is already fully developed. The vision of nature is vividly suggested, contrasting in its magnificence with the cringing and self-ashamed hideousness of the hero. The characters are powerfully sketched in their physical personality with a few harsh touches. The stifling rites of bourgeois existence imprison in a strait jacket the latest paganism of those who dare not rebel against them. The tone of the novelist is one of satire blended with pity and enhanced by poetry.

Genitrix (1923) is laid in the same setting of a gloomy country house near Bordeaux. Fernand Cazenave is the son of a domineering mother, who eyed his marriage with suspicion and treated his bride with hostility. Her animosity grew when the young woman became pregnant; she feared that her son would then escape her for good. The baby, fortunately, was stillborn, and Cazenave's wife is now dying in a solitary room in the bleak, cold house. Her whole past appears in the mind's eye of the abandoned woman: her melancholy childhood spent in poverty, her marriage to a man older by a good many years who trembles like a little child before his authoritarian mother. He had consented to be lured into wedlock through a futile effort to free himself from the maternal tyranny. But he had never given his wife the slightest joy. 'This body of hers was soon to be consumed by death, and it had not known love. No annihilation in the ecstasy of caresses had prepared her for the eternal dissolution.' She dies. Her memory will henceforth live with her weakling husband; it is so much easier to love the dead, as

Mauriac says somewhere, for they do not annoy us any more. Remorse, bitterness against the engrossing love of his mother who can think only of watching his appetite, his sleep, his clothes, his comfort, and of coddling him as if he were still a little child, and contempt for his own selfishness and avarice now turn him against the triumphant Genitrix. She, who thought she had recaptured her son with the death of her daughter-in-law, now finds herself rejected. She dies in her turn and leaves her son to his solitude. He, like many a man, should have gone through life without even trying to know what love is.

Genitrix is, in its condensed beauty, almost unbearably harsh; the theme of maternal love driven to tyrannical excesses, worthy of Greek tragedy, has seldom been approached by a novelist with such stark courage. The three characters are depicted with cruel truth, unrelieved by any touch of irony or tenderness. The beauty of the flesh and the fond transfiguration of the loved one by the lover have little place in such a novel. Children and domestic animals hardly ever seem to inhabit Mauriac's world. Only the changing seasons or the tragic grandeur of the night, with the whistle of express trains in the distance and the sounds of the owls or the nightingales in the garden, bring a momentary vision of external beauty, contrasting with the feverish emotions of the characters, bent on mutual torture.

Le Désert de l'amour has more ample scope. Not only is the novel longer, with changes in place and time, but it offers a subtle orchestration of diverse themes and varies the novelist's focus by presenting three protagonists of almost equal importance. Dr. Courrèges has led a life of incessant labor; his wife, absorbed by the material worries of daily living, has gradually lost all spiritual companionship with her husband. Professional success has come to him, but he is profoundly lonely. He, who has pierced through the secrets of many patients and listened to their confessions, cannot break through the wall of shyness and misunderstanding that separates him from his own son. The latter, an uncouth and gawky adolescent, frets in the atmosphere of cold suspicion that prevails in the home; he neglects his studies, affects a brutal cynicism, and awaits the experience of love, which might transform him.

When the novel opens, fourteen years after the events, Raymond Courrèges is sitting in a bar in Paris. A woman enters with an older man. He recognizes her as an old acquaintance from Bordeaux, Maria Cross. The train of memories takes him back to his life as a schoolboy of eighteen, when he used to take the evening streetcar back to the suburbs of Bordeaux. On it he met Maria Cross, a woman of doubtful reputation, kept by some rich merchant. Maria Cross was no lady of vice, not even a coquettish or sensuous woman. She had fallen into her existence out of weariness; she harbored sentimental yearnings and became fondly and maternally attached to the clumsy lad who, every evening, sat opposite her in the dingy streetcar. At the same time, his father, the doctor, was falling in love with her, respectfully and naïvely, like a man of science having suddenly, in middle age, discovered romantic tenderness. The woman worshipped the doctor as a saint and fondly accepted the affection of the adolescent until, one afternoon, he brutally tried to rape her. He was repulsed and mocked. Vexed in his male pride and hurt in having been judged both silly and repellent, he left her, eager to take revenge upon other women for the wound inflicted upon his vanity. He embarked on a dissolute life but never would forget or forgive the woman who had treated him like the clumsy child that he was.

The last pages of the volume take us back to the bar in Paris. Maria Cross, after years of a semirespectable liaison, is now married. She has recognized Raymond, vaguely recalled the ridiculous adventure that, for her, never counted. Her husband is suddenly seized by a stroke. And it is the old Dr. Courrèges, who had telegraphed his son that same morning to announce his visit to Paris, who is called by him to attend to the sick man. Father and son briefly meet near the woman whom they both had fondly dreamed of, still vainly trying to understand each other, solitary pilgrims in the desert of love.

A similar technique of relating the events in retrospect, as they flash upon the memory of the chief actor reliving every gesture, every sensation or thought that once was his, is used to superb advantage in *Thérèse Desqueyroux.* The point of view of the protagonist is thus adopted without any artificiality, and the reader shares the sense of solitude that afflicted the heroine, to the point of excusing her criminal attempt. Of all his women characters, Mauriac has drawn Thérèse with the deepest sympathy and with the finest nuances of convincing verisimilitude. Twice he felt impelled to return to the same heroine and perhaps to bring her to God. He shrank, however, before the conversion that might have saved Thérèse in the religious sense but would have imperiled her complex humanity.

Thérèse was a provincial *jeune fille,* the daughter of wealthy proprietors of acres of pines and vineyards, who accepted marriage, with no more love than is customary in such unions, to Bernard Desqueyroux, a landowner who seemed cultured and handsome. But Thérèse finds no happiness in married life, not even in maternity. She reads, thinks, smokes cigarettes, and judges her mediocre husband with lucidity, soon with severity and hostility. He is brutal and animal in his physical seizure of his bride; her senses are repelled by his complacent male coarseness. Every one of his thoughts revolves around the land and the family. Thérèse feels forever imprisoned in a dreary cage. Hatred for her husband creeps into her heart, and fear that her own daughter may have inherited too much of the paternal coarseness and conventionality haunts her.

15

One day, while a fire was raging outside, in the pine forests, Bernard unwittingly pours himself a double dose of the arsenic that had been prescribed for him. She fails to warn him. She then is tempted to pour poison herself for her husband, and she falsifies the doctor's prescription to obtain it. Her husband survives, and her crime is discovered. She is saved from a prison sentence by Bernard's wish that the family be spared such a scandal. She is taken back to her husband's house and sequestered there until, one day, stifling in her prison, she decides to break away and live by herself in Paris. Appearances have been preserved. The family can exult, and Bernard can go back to his truest concerns, those of a landowner, sportsman, and voracious eater.

Thérèse, the sinner, the unbeliever, is the heroine of Mauriac. For she has suffered and revolted; and she is lamentably misunderstood by her middle-class family, who are aghast that one of them should insist upon thinking and acting in her own way. Mauriac delineated her with tender care, while apologizing for not creating characters 'streaming with virtue and pure in heart.' He presented her with the most precious gift a novelist can make to his heroes: he endowed her with mystery. She herself never knew what had impelled her to poison her husband. Shade plays with light, and half-shades with more glaring color in Thérèse, the most subtle and the most pitiful of Mauriac's oppressed women.

Mauriac's most successful novels eschew the confusing turbulence of the fiction in which life seems constantly to erupt with fresh incident and new characters. The novelist's most powerful stories are also the barest. Artistic unity is achieved through our perceiving every detail through the lens of one central character. But our vision remains impartial, for the protagonist who tells the tale is pitiless to his own failings. The form of reminiscences or of a diary occasionally interposes remoteness between the events remembered and the reader, keeping the reader at a distance and in a state of tranquility. In Mauriac's use of the form, on the contrary, the reader is carried away by the torrent overflowing from the tormented heart of the protagonist. The feverish, broken-up style of the interior monologue wins the reader's participation in sordid calculations and venomous hatreds.

Le Noeud de vipères is an artistic masterpiece, somber as a Shakespearean tragedy without comic relief and momentary escape into the ecstasy of the lyric. The hero is a King Lear with no Cordelia at his side, a Balzacian miser without the fierce passion for gold that transfigures Père Grandet. Everything in the middle-class family described by Mauriac is sordid. Jealousy, hatred, spying on one another, lying, and the sadistic infliction of wounds through words poison the family circle, which Mauriac, himself the happiest of family heads, refuses to see in rosy hues. But the true viper's tangle is the heart of the old man, Louis, who has kept a diary for years so that his wife might one day peruse it and marvel at how much he scorned and distrusted her.

Her 'crime' was that she had married him for money, after having broken an earlier engagement into which, presumably, she had poured more sincere feeling than she was ever to experience for her husband Louis. She belonged to an old family, which had lost its fortune, and she thought she honored Louis by accepting his hand, for he was but a son of peasants who had risen through their stubborn thrift. He had received a good education, had worked with zeal to be able to eclipse in intellectual achievement the young men whose greater social ease and worldly success he envied. Succeeded he had, and when he discovered that his bride had married him solely for his position and his money, while scorning his humbler origin and clumsy manners, he was wounded for life. Moneymaking became for him the only joy; or rather, a wild drive for possession of material good replaced in him the affections of the heart. His wife raised their children against him, as her potential allies; she nurtured them in a conformist and Pharisaic religious attitude, which professed horror at the father's unbelief. He lived on in his alienated home, surrounded by children and grandchildren who feared him and who speculated avidly on the amount that the old man was likely to leave them on the day of his death. He, in the bitterness of his heart, fed on revenge and plotted to hand most of his securities to an illegitimate child he had once had and thus deprive his family of the coveted legacy. The scheme is foiled through the cowardice of the bastard son.

His wife, for whom the venomous diary was intended, died before him. To the old man, long starved for affection, who had been waylaid by possessiveness and retaliation for the blows he had suffered early in life, another path now opened. Like most people, he had deceived himself only to be able to live. Hatred and vengeance had been vain pursuits for him. 'I have always been mistaken as to the object of my desires. We do not know what we desire, we do not love what we think we love.' Beneath the vipers entangled in his hardened heart was a nugget of charity. He inscribed in his mournful diary the name of the one true Love; he was drawn to Christ by his sufferings and sins, before he died.

But for its final pages, where the move toward divine charity appears too sudden and unexplained—a common feature of literary works in which supernatural grace invades a soul through an illumination, which can neither be prepared nor accounted for rationally—*Le Noeud de vipères* ranks among the most masterly novels of the century. Within a brief compass and through a voluntarily restricted technical medium, Mauriac has explored depths of evil and potentialities for good in a human creature. He has given concrete form to a vision of life and of man that is dark but is lighted up by charity. Without any elaborate description or ideological digression, he has afforded his reader an insight into social problems proposed by a middle class gnawed by avarice, Pharisaism, conventionality, and relentless selfishness.

Only one other of Mauriac's novels, in our opinion, ranks among his best, and even in that one the flaws are more conspicuous than in the earlier masterpieces, and the emphasis on the Catholic psychology of the characters is overstressed for the non-Catholic reader. The novel is *La Pharisienne* (*A Woman of the Pharisees*). The leading character, Brigitte Pian, is a deeply religious woman who might be called an unconscious or a sincere hypocrite. She forces others to practice virtue and thus drives them to revolt or hatred. She ruins a priest whose faith she finds too weak, dooms a frail young woman who insists upon knowing love of the flesh, [4] and turns her own religion into a caricature of Christian mercy. With his usual subtlety, Mauriac allows us to infer only that impure elements may enter into the making of such an imperious propagandist of enforced virtue, who may combine greed for power over souls, sexual unbalance perhaps, and sincere striving after saintliness. But he refrains from intrusive analysis and from the comments of a moralist. Several paths are opened before the reader down which he may venture to seek an interpretation of the novel. The technique differs from the retrospection or from the diary device of most earlier stories. A narrator is introduced, who participates in the action yet abstracts herself from it at times to interpret it to the readers. Some of the stark unity of Mauriac's more vivid masterpieces is thus lost.

Much in Mauriac must be explained by his determination not to become another Bourget, who preached the validity of Christianity for political and social reasons and praised Catholicism as an adjunct of order and an instrument for discipline. The author of *The Pharisienne* is Catholic but not clerical. Faith is, to him, not a haven of security and serene joy. Good does not reign on earth, and the hearts of the faithful are far remote from the purity of little children. Indeed, St. Francis celebrating the naïve beauty of birds and flowers, and Christ pointing to the lilies of the field are infrequent visitations in modern Catholic literature. Evil lurks behind every shape and perfume that is beautiful; the ultimate descent of grace into disturbed hearts takes place most surely once sin has paved the way to regeneration. Mauriac's Catholic novel insists upon remaining bold and powerful; it is Catholic and Christian because it respects the ugly truth of life and conforms to reality. Its characters are not docile believers bent at will by their creator; they resist him, rebel against being led to Paradise. In a little book written in memory of a friend of his youth who died during World War I, Mauriac clearly defined his purpose: 'A certain literature of edification falsifies life. The transcendence of Christianity appears most manifest in its conformity with reality. Do not then fake reality. To depict man in all his misery is to unmask the abyss opened, in the modern world, by God's absence.' [5]

It is strange that it should be in our time, when faith is less widespread than in the past centuries, that Catholic literature, long relegated to an unenviable place, has regained ascendancy with Péguy, Claudel, Bernanos, Mauriac, and certain Catholic writers of note in England and America. Catholicism, by once more placing disquietude at the core of religious literature, has tapped the sources for a new tragic feeling for life.

The advantages derived by Mauriac from his Catholic conception of the world are to perceive life as unceasingly torn between contrary forces and to picture man as restlessly preyed upon by the powers of Evil. Christianity, says Mauriac, enters into souls in order to divide them.

The world is an arena for the struggle in which the Devil fights against God, vice against virtue, the animal part of ourselves against the call of the spirit. To the honest observer, virtue is not triumphant, as it may be in edifying novels; nor can vice win in the end, for that would be a denial of Providence. Thus a conflict is perpetually being waged. Man finds in his own ability to doom himself the very proof of his freedom. He revolts against God; but the life he makes for himself is, but for a few unreal moments of bodily and sensuous exultation, afflicted with an oppressive sense of dereliction.

Life assumes a significance to the Catholic novelist, in contrast with the naturalist author in whose fiction one felt only the slow, meaningless gnawing of an average existence, abandoned to forces of heredity, environment, and instinct. The Catholic novel portrays a struggle, with an end at least dimly perceived, sometimes attained with the help of divine grace. Sin also takes on a significance.

The Catholic novel rests on a sharp distinction between Good and Evil. Man surrenders to the call of his desires or to the violence of his passions voluntarily and, what is more, fully conscious that he is breaking a moral law. 'La conscience dans le mal' [6] gives added zest to his pleasures, but works for his remorse, and in some cases for his salvation. Mauriac goes much further. Sinning appears in his fiction as the prerequisite for entering through the strait gate and winning 'more room in Heaven' after the sinner will have atoned for the sin by repentance. This concept reassures his disturbed characters that they were not born to the conventional existence of a timid Pharisee; they are not, therefore, incapable of the *élan* that plunges them into hell only to raise them all the more securely into the abode of the elect.

Those who seem vowed to evil were perhaps elect before all others, and the depths of their fall measure the extent to which they have betrayed the task to which they were destined. There would be no blessed in Heaven if they had not received the power to damn themselves; it may be that they alone rush into perdition who might have become saints. [7]

The doctrine is not without its dangers, which moralists could denounce. [8] But it offers unambiguous advantages to the Catholic novelist, who uncovers snares laid by demons in the beauty of an April morning, in the loveliness of a youthful face, in the encounter of a young man and a young woman in a restaurant or on a bathing beach. While Anatole France and many another novelist traditionally called Gallic accepted the pleasures of the flesh as the most valuable adornment of our brief life, Mauriac pictures them as unreal and followed by unspeakable misery. 'Christianity makes no allowance for the flesh; it suppresses it,' asserts our theologian-novelist. And, as he elsewhere adds, we cannot love both Cybele and Christ. Conflict waged against one half of ourselves and vigilance against all in outward nature that could seduce us into paganism give Mauriac's novels a tragic meaningfulness that Epicureans and skeptics seldom achieve in fiction.

Not all Catholic readers feel secure in the presence of such stories of temptation and subsequent remorse. Some openly regret that this Frenchman from the south should be relentlessly oppressed by the vision of sin. They would prefer the harmonious balance between the flesh and the spirit achieved by Hellenic culture and attempted by humanism after its discovery of antiquity. They contrast the hideousness of caresses exchanged between lepers in Mauriac's world with the splendor of the kiss bestowed by Cleopatra on Antony in Shakespeare's play, when the Queen of Egypt, who had mastered the art of sinning with grace, proclaimed herself and her lover peerless before the world. [9] Others, less nonchalant in their tolerance of the charming evils that flesh is heir to, have wondered which of the two phases often described alternately in Mauriac's novels was the more powerfully delineated and the more likely to remain engraved in the memory of young readers: the descent into the abysses of vice, or the ultimate dipping into holy water and the visitation of faith when sinners were no longer able to bear their strenuous life of sin?

Mauriac, in the sincerity of his faith, has pondered over some of these criticisms, of which his coreligionists have not been sparing. But he has remained convinced that his duty is to depict man as he sees him and to describe the world with the truth from which great Christian artists have seldom flinched. 'To dare say everything, but to dare say everything chastely. Not to divorce ardor from purity.' The most unchristian view of life would conceal the power of temptation to carry away the frail and even the most resolute of creatures. Like many Catholics and like many Frenchmen, Mauriac is primarily anti-Rousseau; man, to him, was not born good and can only with much effort become so, seldom through his own light. Not desire and lechery alone, but pride, avarice, bourgeois complacence, hatred of one's neighbors and family, the vanity of petty pleasures, and, most of all, the incurable stupidity of many human beings testify to the pervading influence of original sin. 'Men are all fools,' said another Catholic, an Englishman, G. K. Chesterton. 'This doctrine is sometimes called the doctrine of original sin. It may also be described as the natural equality of man.'

Mauriac's originality as a novelist lies in his Catholic vision of the world, in his analysis of love and especially of middle-aged women and adolescents led by a love affair to explore the bitter depths of love. It lies, too, in his craftsmanship, which, conscious and subtle as it is, contrives to leave in the novel the element by which it is most likely to challenge time—poetry.

Love hallowed by the sacrament of marriage and embellished by the devotion of the Christian couple to the service of God is hardly a theme for Catholic novelists. Happiness does not interest a creator. The radiating joy of lovers who might find an absolute in physical love is the foe Mauriac pursues relentlessly, either in the second act of *Tristan und Isolde,* where, to Mauriac's relief, the lovers' raptures can end only in death, or in *Lady Chatterley's Lover,* against which he has shot the arrows of his bitterest irony, in 'Eros,' *Journal I* and 'Une Gorgée de poison,' *Journal II.* To him, desire is always hideous. 'It transforms the person who draws near us into a monster that is no longer like him. Nothing then stands any longer between us and our accomplice.' His married women have, of course, ceased to expect any pleasure or joy. No mutual esteem, no admiration ever precedes or prolongs physical love. Love is nothing but a delusion that makes us feel our loneliness more acutely, or a fleeting sadistic impulse to humiliate our partner. More often still, with Mauriac, love is the inordinate power to torment us with which we have suddenly invested another creature. 'There's beggary in the love that can be reckoned',' whispered Shakespeare's Antony. The French novelist, listening to Wagner's opera, mourns: 'How can love ever be reckoned, except by the tears that we draw from our partner?'

Mauriac indicts the flesh because he fears its power. Like the ascetics, he brands its pleasures as lamentably brief and preposterously vain, since they rest on illusions about our partner and delusions about ourselves. Love cannot live on if the lovers renounce the martyrdom of separation. Let lovers understand their true role, which is that of being the executioner of one another, he exclaims in a very pregnant preface to *Trois Récits* (1929). Human love will fill its only true purpose if it serves as a tool to inflict suffering upon us, a hook to catch us unawares and lift us to the only love that disappoints not —divine love.

His partial view of passion, his denial of the mere possibility of happiness illustrates the limitations of Mauriac. He never aimed at universality and he did not claim objectivity. 'The novel does not reproduce reality; it transposes it' is one of the many lucid remarks made by the novelist on his art. The novel falsifies life for many a technical reason: for example, it cannot render silences, and must resort to dialogues far more than we do in life; and no fictional device is perhaps more artificial than the much-vaunted interior monologue, in which the novelist conceals his intervention and blends confusedly the perception of a series of events and the consciousness of such a perception. Mauriac cannot hold the mirror up to nature because he starts from an a priori vision of the world. The word metaphysician recurs in critical essays devoted to Mauriac, who is nevertheless hardly a philosophical mind, and he has used it himself in the most fitting characterization that he has made of himself in *Journal II*: 'I am a metaphysician working on the concrete. Owing to a certain gift of atmosphere, I try to make the Catholic universe of evil perceptible, tangible, odorous. The theologians give us an abstract idea of the sinner; I give him flesh and blood.'

Not only must he resort to exaggeration and distortion but he must (or so Mauriac thinks) focus his lens on the inner man and on the isolated individual. Even the portrayal of a family is, with Mauriac, the portrayal of divergent members of one group, impatiently fretting at the prison where they must gather for meals or for the evening rest. They hardly ever communicate. Mauriac repeatedly contended that factory workers do not differ from duchesses in the quality or the manner of their feeling and that love and hatred are fundamentally the same in a farmer's daughter and in Racine's Hermione. He does not attempt to delineate groups or a whole society. He says of himself and of novelists in general, we 'can only depict with some adequacy beings oppressed by a law. . . . The art of the novelist is a bankruptcy.'

Brevity is another self-imposed limitation with him. It keeps him from gaining for his stories the slow collaboration of time. The effect of the corrosion of the years on his characters does not interest Mauriac any more than it did the French tragic writers of the classical age. His manner, to use the Jamesian terminology, is not panoramic (except when characters survey their remembered past) and it is seldom dramatic in the literal sense, for there is very little drama enacted in the presence of the reader. Several of the best novels begin after the climax of the action has been reached, after Raymond Courrèges has lived his life of futility, after Thérèse has been judged for her attempt at poisoning, and after Louis has undone some of the viper's coils oppressing his heart. The passing of time matters less for Mauriac than the exploration in depth of the inner man. Variety in his gallery of characters matters less for him than grappling repeatedly with a few stubborn souls and unearthing more of their secrets.

Sartre, in a scathing article, has pitilessly pointed out the truest weakness of Mauriac: the absence of freedom in his characters. Everything in them is predetermined by heredity, by the curse of original sin, and by their creator or by God. Mauriac once defined the novelist as 'the ape of God.' Sartre concludes his article with the oft-quoted words: 'God is no artist. Neither is Mauriac.' He charges Mauriac with first identifying himself with his characters, then suddenly forsaking them in order to act as a stern judge. Like God, he decrees that his wretched creatures be such and such, but he does not show them in the process of becoming what they are to be. The reader is not uncertain enough about the fate that will ultimately be meted out to them. The element of indetermination, which Sartre, the philosopher and the novelist of freedom, boasts of having restored to fictional characters, is indeed woefully lacking in Mauriac.

But he has other gifts, which compensate those he may lack: that of the tragic writer, hasty, feverish, eager to integrate the discoveries made by Doestoevski and Freud into the French mold of strict construction and swift, unrelenting ardor; that of the moralist, whose concern is to bring to light the still-unexplored or dark recesses of the human heart and to explore the perilous force of passions; above all others, that of the poet. In an interview with Frédéric Lefèvre, Mauriac indirectly hinted at his finest achievement when he declared:

There is little danger in the novel's invading the rest of literature. I believe that only poetry counts, and that only through the poetical elements enclosed in a work of art of any genre whatever does that work deserve to last. A great novelist is first of all a great poet. Both Proust and Tolstoy were because their power of suggestion was boundless.

NOTES

1 The French word is nobler or more pretentious—*la vertu*. Nietzsche scathingly remarked somewhere how the term that used to denote the virile courage of man had been degraded to signify a 'merely negative' attribute of some women.

2 Preface to *Petits Essais de psychologie religieuse* (Société littéraire de France; 1920), written during Mauriac's service on the Eastern front.

3 Mauriac, broad-minded and often unorthodox Catholic that he is, has confessed to a curious fondness for Nietzsche. He wrote in *Le Bâillon dénoué* (Grasset, 1946) that 'no philosopher had remained dearer to him than Nietzsche, the poor antichrist' and that, although Voltaire always repelled him, he counted more than one friend in the posterity of Voltaire: Stendhal, for example, and Giraudoux on whom the Voltairian smile, no longer 'hideous,' sat like a radiant light.

4 Mauriac lends to the narrator of the story in *La Pharis-ienne* the following words, which reveal one of his obsessions and explain the ardent and constant attraction and repulsion that the theme of love holds for him: 'I believe that all the miseries of our human conditions spring from our inability to remain chaste and that human beings vowed to chastity would not be afflicted with most of the evils that oppress them.'

5 *La Vie et la mort d'un poète* (André Lafont), Bloud et Gay, Paris, 1924, p. 32.

6 The line concludes one of the darkest poems in *Les Fleurs du mal*, 'L'Irrémédiable.' Mauriac's affinities with Baudelaire can hardly be exaggerated.

7 Mauriac, *The Mask of Innocence* (Farrar, Strauss and Young, New York, 1953, p. 138).

8 Indeed, a moralist had denounced the doctrine in the second century A.D., for the view that sin gives the sinner a moral superiority and a prior claim to the Kingdom of Heaven is as ancient as Christianity—the pagan apologist Celsus, as reported by Origen in *Contra Celsum*.

9 The criticism was offered with others, in an ironic, yet sympathetic, speech delivered by André Chaumeix when he received Mauriac into the French Academy (November 17, 1933).

Michael F. Moloney

THE WAY OF PASCAL

Few writers have been so frank as François Mauriac in acknowledging their literary and ideological derivations. The chapter headings of his *Mes Grands Hommes* (translated into English as *Men I Hold Great*) contain the names of Pascal, Molière, Voltaire, Rousseau, Chateaubriand, Maurice and Eugénie de Guérin, Balzac, Flaubert, Loti, Barrès, Gide, Radiguet, and Graham Greene. That volume, however, does not fully define the literary influences to which Mauriac has been subjected. Scattered through the journals and critical essays are other names to which, whether in admission of indebtedness or in frank crossing of swords, he returns again and again. Montaigne, Racine, Bazin, Jammes, Lafon, D. H. Lawrence, Dostoievski, Proust, Claudel, Colette—the list is impressive and revealing. Racine, Proust, and Lafon have provoked studies, Gide a retort, Barrès a tribute, Claudel a *réponse*. But in the whole galaxy — largely Gallic, for Mauriac is consistently nationalistic in orientation — it was Pascal more than any other who determined the spirit of his own work. It was the abbé Péquignot, professor of rhetoric at the Marinist college on the outskirts of Bordeaux where so much of his future was shaped, who introduced the young Mauriac to Pascal and since that time, he confesses, the Brunschvieg edition of Pascal has never left him. [1] To the truth of that confession the whole body of his writing bears witness.

The first effect of the intervention of Pascal was to give to Mauriac's religious faith an essential intellectual respectability. To a novelist whose religious convictions are the warp upon which the fabric of his art is woven the significance of this fact is obvious. Few men can have been more sensitive than he to the isolation to which his Catholicism subjected him in the closing years of the nineteenth century and the opening of the twentieth. The mind of the young Christian intellectual in such an epoch, he declares in a passage clearly autobiographical, senses the spirit of denial in the modern world even before he has been predisposed to doubt by philosophic argument or literary experience or the appeal of amorous adventure. The body of believers are themselves a source of scandal to him. He is repelled by the evidence they supply of ". . . intellectual poverty, base credulity, hatred, the fear of strange alluring passions, and, under the guise of edification, prejudice against the most noble works in favor of false and foolish rhapsodies." [2] On the other hand he admires the *savants* and is attracted by the daring speculations and unbridled curiosity of renowned authors who speak for the exigencies of the human heart. The service of Pascal to the young believer so circumstanced is to reveal to him profound spiritual affirmation in one susceptible like himself to the dual tug of carnal temptation and ambition. At such a juncture youth can establish a bond with Pascal if it sees him ". . . as he really was, before his conversion . . ." for however singular Pascal may have been in nature, endowment, and achievement, this great Christian soul remains a ". . . brother in intellectual pride and even in a certain attraction that the passions had for him." [3]

The impact of Pascal's spiritual history, a powerful

shaping influence on Mauriac's personal development as the ubiquitous references in the journals and essays testify, had, unquestionably, a tonal effect upon the novels. More immediately significant, however, was Mauriac's discovery in Pascal of a humanism which, while rejecting nothing of the wide-ranging curiosity of Montaigne, actually complemented Montagne's probing of the mind and heart of man by adding a neglected dimension. Montaigne he recognizes as the true begetter of contemporary humanism—the Montaigne who spent his life in self-analysis, who had seemingly no other concern than accurately to report himself. But to Montaigne the Christian idea of interior progress, of self-perfection was in itself obnoxious. [4] Pascal, no less concerned with man than was Montaigne, is, for Mauriac, the advocate of a profounder humanism, for denying nothing of human nature he would employ the totality of man to attain God. [5] He is the great prototype of a Christian humanism which accepts man as a point of departure but man already touched with the divine. [6] The largeness of Pascal's sympathy revealed itself in his solicitude even for the inheritors of Montaigne. Pascal knew that Montaigne spoke not only for himself but for an innumerable family of kindred spirits, who, believing that it is possible to come to terms with nature and recognizing her complexity, accept her as she is. Very far from viewing man's situation as tragic they immerse themselves in the temporal order and draw therefrom a certain modest happiness. It was the mission of Pascal to disturb the self-satisfaction of these sons of Montaigne, to bring them, anterior to any concern with Revelation, evidences within themselves of rejection, of reprobation, of redemption, in the manner in which the geologist deciphers the earth and thanks to methodical excavations, reconstitutes prehistory. [7]

In *Bordeaux ou l'adolescence*, in *Les Maisons fugitives*, in *Le Jeune homme*, but particularly in *The Frontenac*

Mystery Mauriac has spoken with disarming intimacy of the spiritual perturbation of his own youth. In this period, when the aesthetic impressionability of the budding artist awakened into a tortured conflict with the sentimental Catholicism which he had absorbed at home and at the college of the Grand-Lebrun, Mauriac found the breadth of Pascal's understanding irresistible. The Pascal who could defend both Epictetus and Montaigne before M. de Saci was a fortunate ally for the collegian so deeply impressed at once with the grandeur and misery of human nature. [8] The young Mauriac, already troubled by his dreams of a literary future, so sensitive, as the journals and the early novels reveal, to the kingdoms of the earth and their glory, needed the vision of a life at once humanistic and religious, if he was to follow the ambivalent bent of his inner self. This vision Pascal supplied him. He learned that the sternness of Pascal's religious beliefs and the dolour they entailed had not isolated him from other men. Rather, his spiritual suffering had given Pascal a conviction of the companionship of pain which all men share. He was spared the solitude of despair because he had climbed the rugged path to Calvary, that least solitary of the world's eminences, and there had mingled in the press of those awaiting at the foot of the Cross the final consummation. The spiritual ordeal of Pascal actually rendered him more responsive to human fellowship, Mauriac insists, since, incapable as he was of abstract theological speculation, this great genius took to himself the particular concerns of ordinary Christians. It was not actually the prodigious *esprit* by which he dominated inferior minds that led him to sanctity. No more was it the knowledge of man or the curiosity for all things human which he pushed so far. The secret of his spiritual growth was a charity which he possessed in common with the humblest of men. Hence he is the brother of all sinners, of all converts, of all those disturbed by a spiritual wound which at any moment may bleed afresh. He is in the number of those whom Love has pursued from afar and whose only reliance is that Love. [9]

Thanks to Pascal, then, the human adventure for Mauriac is inextricably involved with the Divine. [10] To those who deny any awareness of an interior exigency, any inner consciousness of the Divine Presence, he grants their probity, but insists that at the beginning of their intellectual and moral histories there was a deliberate rejection of the supernatural. As a result their very reasoning processes proceed from a negation. Their initial passionate repudiation of all transcendentals sufficiently explains their specific insensibility to the things of God. They have in advance obstructed all the channels whereby Grace could reach them. Yet, though nothing less than a lightning bolt such as felled St. Paul on the Damascus road can thereafter reintroduce the supernatural into such lives, even the most indifferent still betray a hunger, however disguised the form of that hunger may be. To escape from God they attempt to find in themselves the equivalent of God, attributing their inmost aspirations to the potentialities of the human spirit. While the world today makes much of repression of the lower instincts in the Freudian sense, the repression of the hunger for God is omnipresent. [11]

In the wake of Pascal the fundamental fact of human life is, for Mauriac, the collision of the Christian ethic with the inclinations of nature. The Christian is committed to a perpetual struggle. The concupiscence of the flesh and the pride of life are twin rivers of fire which he must breast. [12] The whole nobility of man consists in vanquishing his nature where God demands that it should be vanquished. [13] Hence there is an essential difference, Mauriac insists, ". . . between the Christian who resists the life of Grace—that is to say, the sinner—and the religionless man who gives in to the corruption of his nature. The latter thinks he can put corruption inside borders and integrate it into a normal and honorable worldly life. But the sinner knows with a knowledge that comes from God that he will not have done anything towards his salvation if he does not cut off the growth of evil at the root. . . ." [14] The modern age is dominated, he declares, as no other has been, by the religionless man. Modern man, far more than the Romantics, is the son and heir of Rousseau. The Romantics, for all their excesses, were "corrupt children of Christ" holding strongly to the old distinction between good and evil, even though they ". . . exalted evil and played the parts of fallen angels." But today there are many ". . . who force themselves to accept themselves as they are, as Rousseau did." [15] Rousseau has triumphed in the contemporary world, he has become one with its spokesmen. Today ". . . his name is Romain Rolland, Marcel Proust, André Gide. Entire pages of the *Confessions* or *Reveries* could be inserted into *Swann's Way* without it being easy to detect the fraud." [16] The weakness of Proust (who was his friend and for whose art he has expressed a high admiration) as an analyst of the human heart lies for Mauriac in Proust's blindness to the spiritual overtones of human existence. Faith and aspiration, he asserts, are as intimate a part of man's nature as the most evil passions. The gift of self, the search for purity and perfection, the hunger and thirst after justice—to these because they, too, are of the human patrimony, the novelist must render testimony. Why, he asks, do we not accept these as authentic in man as we do the eddies of sensuality and the most obscure heredities? The work of the Christian Dostoievski surpasses that of Proust just because he has seen in his criminals and prostitutes beings fallen, indeed, but also redeemed. God, on the contrary, ". . . is terribly absent . . ." from the world of Marcel Proust whose psychological subtlety commands admiration but whose neglect of the human conscience distorts his view of life. [17]

Here, it would seem, Mauriac is describing by anticipation his own particular significance as a writer of fic-

tion. His many gifts of style, his amazing sensuous awareness, must, in any critical evaluation of the French novel
in the twentieth century, be subordinated to the fact that
it was his undeviating practice to impregnate the novel of
naturalism with the agitated Pascalian concern with sin.
"I flatter myself," he writes in the preface to *Trois récits,*
"that I have painted a world in revolt against the tribunal
of conscience, a miserable world, emptied of Grace." [18]
In so doing he was not actually breaking a new path. The
revival of the Christian concept of sin in French literature
goes back at least to Baudelaire as T. S. Eliot noted in an
essay published thirty years ago. Significantly, Mauriac
recognizes in Baudelaire a spiritual brother. A man of far
purer life, Taine, for example, he declares ". . . is not of
our spiritual family but the miserable Baudelaire is one
of us . . . " and he proceeds to quote Péguy's famous
declaration that the sinner and the saint are equally a part
of Christianity. [19] As a Catholic novelist it is inevitable
that he should be associated with his contemporaries,
Bloy and Bernanos. But, whereas for Bernanos the nature of the naturalists pales before the supernatural and
for Bloy nature is an ordure which the supernatural in
man transcends, Mauriac remains within the naturalistic
tradition while insisting that nature to escape caricature
must not only admit the mysterious impingement of the
supernatural but accept this impingement as its own inevitable fulfillment. Proust, retaining the general contours
of the physical world of Zola, has concerned himself
largely with the subterranean psychic pressures and erup-
tions which give that world its topography. Mauriac, although accepting his brilliant artistry, maintains that, with
all his passionate sensitivity, Proust has still failed to por-
tray the ultimate potentiality of man. He has made his
own the task which he insists is primarily incumbent on
those who would follow Proust into the hitherto unknown
psychological lands Proust has explored—the task of in-
tegrating Grace in these new worlds. [20]

His conviction of man's radical insufficiency, of what he himself calls "the sense of human feebleness" follows logically from Mauriac's spiritual premises. Whereas the humanist seems to have always before his eyes the image of an abstract man, strong, self-sufficient, invulnerable, the Christian, he suggests, sees the immensity of human misery. One of the greatest obstacles that confront Christianity in the modern world is the loss, especially among intellectuals, of this sense of human weakness. The stoic virtue of the humanist is based on the desperate lie that it is necessary to present an unyielding front not only against sickness, old age, infidelities, treasons, even against death itself, but especially against the defections of the soul, against the appetites which man gratifies in secret, against the immense degradation which from adolescence to senility overwhelms him. The logic of his position leads the humanist ultimately to deny that degradation is degradation, that evil is evil. [21] But the Christian, he continues, far from insisting on man's superiority to suffering, knows, however the humanist may deny it, that in every life there is an individual cross on which each in his turn, soon or late, must stretch himself out. [22] The Christian vocation is a vocation to suffering. The saints, the ". . . great solitary eagles . . . ," such as John of the Cross, ". . . soar far above the crowd and draw other chosen eagles in their wake. But God hides in the midst of cities, according to the needs of each age, among less sublime creatures who love, suffer, and expiate close to the ground, at man's height, and finally, the humblest rejoin the most sublime in the same nudity, in the same joy." [23]

It is this vocation to suffering which for Mauriac gives particular meaning to human life. To flee sorrow and to evade one's cross is the concern of the world, but that concern ". . . is at the same time a fleeing from one's own self and a losing of one's own self, for our special aspect is given us by our sorrow and our special contours are

36

fixed and checked by our cross." [24] Many of Mauriac's readers, even those inclined to sympathize with his basic view of life, have been repelled by what they feel is the harshness of his vision. Bluntly he insists, ". . . the people who look for comfort and consolation and ease in their religion clutter up the threshold without entering the building." [25] The true force of Christianity does not lie for him in its power to exempt man from suffering but rather in its ability to give meaning to suffering. The Christian knows why he suffers. In imitation of his crucified God and in union with Him, he has a part in His agony, he cooperates in the redemption of the world. [26] Participation in that high privilege demands of the Christian the stripping of self which alone sanctifies all suffering. The frequency with which he quotes Pascal's "Lord, I give You all," indicates Mauriac's emphasis on that complete detachment from self and from other creatures which is the price of spiritual growth.

Obviously, the omnipresence of spiritual struggle has given to Mauriac's novels their identifying character. That is a principal reason why Georges Hourdin can say justly that all his characters have a family resemblance, that he seems always to have written the same novel. [27] It explains, too, Alain Palante's observation that in the most suffocating atmosphere of evil, Mauriac surrounds man with the divine. [28] Similarly, Ramon Fernandez has noted that whether his characters are ostensibly concerned with God or not they cannot escape Him. [29] The latter critic has also pointed to a further narrowing effect in Mauriac's work. For him the infinite possibilities present in the temporal-eternal conflict within man have been reduced to the unending dichotomy of spirit and flesh. [30] The whole drama of human existence, as he portrays it, is here concentrated. The bitterness of this internal strife is intensified for Mauriac because, however sharply he may condemn the vulgarization of Freud and the other psychologists of the unconscious, [31] he has been profoundly influenced by them. Even they in their exploitation of the subliminal world, have not gone beyond the novelist who can write: "Passions whether collective . . . or individual are at the source of all that is inspired." [32] The same passions, he insists, can lead man to infamy and degradation or launch him on the divine quest, for there is only one love. [33]

Although man, in Mauriac's view, can never escape his sense of divine filiation, his earthly pilgrimage is fixed in an environment which openly conspires with the inclinations of his physical nature. The earth from which he springs bespeaks the pagan deities rather than the Christian God. This paganism which looms large in all of the novels is not necessarily sinister, although always potentially so. Mauriac, as a Catholic, finds the conflict of earthly-inspired passions and grace inescapable. As a poet whose senses are keenly alert to the aching beauty of the universe he knows that myriads of his fellow men treasure a nostalgic attraction to that beauty. In *Bonheur du chrétien* he relates how his mother, a few minutes before she died, pointed to the landscape outside her window and exclaimed, "It is this that I shall miss. . . ." She did not doubt that in the future life she would be reunited to her children ". . . but she could not conceive the existence of another light to which the brightness of this beautiful day of her death would be as darkness. . . ." [34] Even when the call of the earth is not a source of moral perturbation, it competes with the Divine for the suffrage of man's heart. The love which old Gormac and his daughter-in-law share for their vines and pines was "their sacrament of worship," [35] a manifestation of their hunger for stability in the midst of flux. Rarely, however, is the earth so neutral in its appeal. Most often it is conceived as the realm of Cybele, the implacable goddess whose service cannot be reconciled with that of Christ, who has more worshippers in France than Christ. [36] There was one moment in the history of the world, the dawn of the thirteenth century, when men thought that Christ, in the person of St. Francis of Assisi, had exorcised nature— "The branches crackled under the flight of the last centaur, saints of both sexes replaced the nymphs of the springs, and humanity could believe that the prophetic cry heard one night on the sea—'The great Pan is dead,'— had been fulfilled." But centuries later, at the renaissance, the ancient gods returned, if only in partial triumph. "They returned but God remains." [37]

Here, then, is the particularization of the Mauriacien drama, the fact that in the internal struggle which rends man's soul the external universe participates on the side of the carnal inclinations. Because the struggle is internal, the actions of Mauriac's novels are uncomplicated and the settings are, for the most part, in the village or countryside. Strangely, on the pavements of the great city the drama of the flesh is muted. In Paris, he holds, the very exploitation of sexual love is a source of its alienation—where there are so many appeals scarcely one is heard. But in the silence of the country man truly knows the call of the flesh. Here ". . . universal desire is evident: the cloud of pollen in the air, the amorous vibration of the meadow, the branch above your head which bends beneath the weight of two birds, and, if your maid is young, the garden at night thronged with young men. . . .[38]

If it was Pascal who showed Mauriac how inextricably man is caught up in a warfare of two worlds, it was Maurice de Guérin who established for him this precise milieu of his own Pascalian conflict. For most English-speaking readers who know him at all, de Guérin is the subject of an essay which Matthew Arnold included in the first *Essays in Criticism* of 1865. Arnold, in his desire to dispel the insularity of English letters, introduced into the same volume essays on Heine and Joubert and an-

other on de Guérin's sister, Eugénie. Just why he was
attracted to de Guérin, aside from the fact that Sainte-
Beuve had introduced him into two *Causeries* is not wholly evident. He quotes liberally from de Guérin's journal
and the prose poem, *Centaur,* noting duly the author's
interest in the circle of Lamennais at la Chênai and his
effort in his creative work to "make magically near and
real the life of Nature." He sees in de Guérin a French
Keats, distinguishing, however, Keats' "sense of what is
pleasurable and open in the life of Nature," from de
Guérin's "sense of what there is adorable and secret in
the life of Nature." This latter tantalizing distinction which
Arnold does not develop is a fitting introduction to
Mauriac's commentary.

In the first volume of his own journal Mauriac confesses that his adolescent reading of de Guérin's journal
established their fellowship. [39] Later he specifies the extent of that intimacy: "He is our youth. He is at once our
self and the friend we loved. . . . He offers us . . . the
image of a nobility and grace unknown in the crass
century in which we are condemned to live." [40] While
the eloquence of the la Chênaie group was to lose its appeal for Mauriac—". . . as we advance in years, we prefer silence" [41]—there is no reason to believe that the appeal of de Guérin himself ever lessened. It was de Guérin
who initiated him into the silent passions of the earth.
"He gave to our weak and wavering adolescence the in-
toxicating certainty of being the consciousness of the
vegetable creation. It was in us that the trees tortured by
the west wind, the hills darkened by the shadow of a
cloud, became aware of themselves." [42] Obviously, de
Guérin is here for Mauriac a potential St. Francis. Yet
the synthesis of the natural and the supernatural toward
which de Guérin struggled was only imperfectly achieved.
He was never able, says Mauriac, to assign to nature a
Cyrenaic role in his dolorous way. Death alone could

reconcile for him his love of the Creator and of the world created. [43] This dual attraction so vividly realized in de Guérin is for Mauriac the common heritage of Christians.

Following de Guérin, Mauriac is a poet-novelist smitten with the beauty of the physical universe, yet never losing contact with the mysteries of the human heart which are inextricably bound up with that universe. For him it is at once man's burden and his glory that he cannot identify himself with the earth to which he is so deeply attracted. Human life is basically tragic, the tragedy lodging in the circumstance that man, a creature of two worlds, cannot rest in the one nor apparently attain the other. The struggle to reconcile the two worlds, as befits tragedy, always ends in failure.

How deeply Mauriac was himself involved in the conflict he has made the center of his creative endeavor he has indicated in *Souffrances et bonheur de chrétien*, but the proper introduction to these essays is *God and Mammon*, published in 1929, the same year as *Bonheur* and a year after *Souffrances*. Mauriac early in life was convinced that he could never escape the Catholicism into which he had been born. Still, the very conviction of the inevitability of his religious position called for an effort to evade its bonds. He writes that from the age of sixteen he revolted against the pious practices of his family and masters and against the behavior of the priests who came to his home, indulging to the full all his critical inclinations.

Nature slowly gained the ascendancy over grace. I despaired of re-establishing a balance between them, and I saw these two enemy powers arrayed irrevocably one against the other. My God did not want to let my thoughts dwell, even for a moment, on what my passions dictated. Then who, who (an evil spirit whispered to me), who of the people around me practised this pitiless, merciless doctrine? Hardly anybody; and several people who did, several who had embraced the *folly of the cross*, I found dying of thirst by the very water

41

which is supposed to quench all thirst; and other adherents who were satisfied I explained away by saying that they had never felt any thirst. [44]

This is the proper background for *Souffrances du pécheur* [45] of which the opening paragraphs are probably the most significant for an understanding of the novels.

Christianty makes no provision for the flesh. It suppresses it. 'God wants all,' Bossuet wrote, and Pascal: 'Lord, I give you all.'

It is true that marriage is a sacrament. But Christian marriage, in condemning the wife to perpetual fecundity, condemns the husbands to perpetual chastity. 'The basest condition of Christianity,' Pascal wrote of marriage, 'vile and prejudicial according to God.' And Bossuet is more terrible still. 'Sordid from our birth and conceived in iniquity,' he writes to Mme. Cornuau, 'conceived in the heat of a brutal concupiscence, in the revolt of the senses and in the extinction of reason, we must struggle even to death against the evil which is born with us.' [46]

Six months after the appearance of *Souffrances* Mauriac published his "retraction" in *Bonheur du chrétien*. The heart of the "retraction" appears early in the treatise.

The abuse of human logic in things divine is the error of Jansenism. . . . I have made it my concern to cast into shadow all the pathways traced by loving Grace and the retreats sacred to the nourishment and repose of souls. I did not deny the truth, but I denied that it was accessible. In consequence *Souffrances du chrétien* testifies to my obstinacy in making enemies of the spirit and flesh, neither of which, I said, can live without the destruction of the other.

This was the daring presumption of a man who reads the words of eternal life and interprets them as he desires rather than adapting his ephemeral life to them.

The man accuses the Author of life of failing to make provision for the flesh and the Author of life takes vengeance by overwhelming this soul and this body in his love to the point that he confesses the law of the spirit to be, indeed, the law of the flesh. [47]

42

Mauriac's friend, Charles Du Bos, has insisted upon the significance of *Bonheur du chrétien* as the record of a conversion following close on the heels of *Souffrances*, [48] a point of view frequently supported by Mauriac's own language. Yet "conversion" would scarcely seem to be the accurate word. In *Encore le bonheur,* the sequel to *Bonheur du chrétien,* Mauriac restates with all the old poignancy, the sharpness of the struggle to which man is heir—

External distractions divert us not only from the good but from the evil as well. The thousand incidents of Parisian life turn our attention from the beast within whom we never completely subdue. . . . But in solitude man and his familiar beast remain face to face not for an hour only but for days and nights on end. It is then that the faithful soul who had believed he had progressed far discovers with anguish that he is at the point of departure. An infinite bounty has seized him, as an inert prey, tearing him from the claws and muzzle of the beast. This all powerful friend strengthens him against succumbing to the fascination of the fixed and dismal eyes of the beast who, hungry but unhurried, lurks nearby. All around the abandoned countryside sleeps, delivering itself to the south wind, to the blustering rain, to sun and shadow, with no suggestion of resistance. The living body mimics this passivity until a breath on its face announces the raging beast is at hand, and there is time only to murmur the words of salvation: *Domine, ad adjuvandum me festina.* [49]

Du Bos, consistent with his theory, hailed *That Which Was Lost* as signalizing a new direction in Mauriac's art through the elimination of all "connivance" on the author's part. Every creature, every state of body and soul, every sensation is in this novel presented such as it is and not otherwise, Du Bos declared. The bath of sensations, the lyric halo which in the earlier novels enveloped and illumined a turbulent nature have been succeeded by the "austere beauty of an art of fugue." [50] Du Bos, it is true, wrote at a time when *That Which Was Lost* and *Vipers' Tangle* were the sole fruits of the supposed conversion. Yet in the relatively late *The Unknown Sea* and *The Loved and*

Unloved, and even in *The Frontenac Mystery* and *The Mask of Innocence,* Mauriac not only handles the same essential theme, the conflict between the naturalistic and Christian concepts of love, between Cybele and Christ, but does so with more than a hint of the connivance of the earlier manner. There is no dearth of passages in *The Unknown Sea* and *The Loved and Unloved* where rich sensuous descriptions are employed to create a compliant tropical luxuriance of background against which passionate young love plays itself out. While the hothouse atmosphere of *Destinies* and *The Desert of Love* is never again wholly reproduced, the difference in tone of the later novels would seem to be explicable rather by the fact that middle age and after is rarely productive of the lyric manner than by any conscientious scruple. Here North is much nearer the truth when he questions the reorientation of the artist in Mauriac after 1929. He agrees that Mauriac, at that time, made a great advance in the knowledge of his faith, an advance which is shown in his religious essays and in his journalism. The creative writer, however, he thinks was little affected. Although he was henceforth to reject certain subjects, the approach to life in the novels remains unchanged. [51] From this point of view *Souffrances* and *Bonheur* may logically be accepted not as the definitively negative and positive poles of Mauriac's Catholicism, the rebellious rejection and the duly recited submission, but as a public debate with himself. In *Souffrances* he stresses the difficulty of Christian conformance. In *Bonheur* he emphasizes the joys of the victory which man's will strengthened by Grace can achieve over his earthly-directed passions. The debate did not end with the publication of *Bonheur.* Had it so terminated Mauriac's art would have been at an end. It was the argumentative cast of *Souffrances* which caused many readers to identify its sentiments with its author and forced him to an answer. But the sufferings of the Christian soul brought to bay by temptations and the ascetic joy of their rejection have been from the beginning and have remained the constant focus of Mauriac's fictional effort.

For the student of the novels Mauriac's spiritual history introduces questions concerning the manner of his handling of his central theme. Has he, as has been charged, with his Pascalian insistence on the inevitability of spiritual conflict, posed for his characters, in the Pascalian manner, an unfair dilemma? Has he committed man to a struggle against his corrupted nature which he is predestined to lose? Such misgivings have perturbed many of his admirers and with good reason. Palante has gone further than any other critic in accusing Mauriac of invoking impossible odds against his men and women. The choice which Mauriac offers, he declares, is not really free. The novel of Mauriac when it evokes the passions is the novel of physical predestination. [52] Still others have stressed the part which inheritance plays in the destiny of Mauriac's characters [53] and the works themselves, fictional and non-fictional, provide, on the surface at least, ample documentation of Palante's judgment. Thus in the "pre-conversion" *Souffrances du pécheur,* commenting on Bossuet's insistence that the perverse human will alone is responsible for man's reprobation, Mauriac observes that Bossuet never asks whether each of us appears to the Eternal Being as an individual or as the moment of a race. Then, declaring that he does not seek to equivocate but accepts the doctrine of free will in all its rigor, he goes on to insist that even so man carries within him more than himself, that the individual is not merely a divided man, as the Apostle believed, but many men. "The sinner in himself is a myth. He is, in reality, an accumulation of inherited tendencies." Certainly, he admits the existence of the morally responsible person whom each man creates within himself, but the wastes left over from that creation continue to live and exude their poisons. [54] In *God and Mammon* where he is defending himself against André

Gide's subtle sneers at his making the best of two worlds he dilates upon the unbroken chain which connects the man of middle age with his childhood and the child with his racial past. The life of man, he asserts ". . . is a tightly woven web, and no power in the world can interrupt the unrolling of it, and no scene of the drama it unweaves can be detached or put aside." Moreover, if man ". . . wishes to go further back than childhood and reach the very source of his fate, he may see it leaping from the womb of the earth, poisoned even then with all the substances which poison it today." [55] In the "post-conversion" *Les Maisons fugitives* he affirms that with or without his own destiny would have been unchanged. "The man we are exists essentially from the beginning. Freely or across a thousand obstacles we attain him." [56]

The novels abound in illustrations of natural fatality. The basic weakness of *Le Fleuve de feu* lies in the fact that the fall of Gisèle de Plailly is made to depend solely upon what Lucille de Villeron calls her "mortal predestination." It is true that Mauriac now finds interesting in that novel only the descriptive presentations of the opening pages but the weakness of the plot which leaves Gisèles's two love affairs only superficially motivated is a dramatic example of the extent to which, even in the beginning of his mature period, he felt that character is destiny. Maria Cross, drifting into her attachment with young Courrèges, feels the reprehensibility of her actions but is powerless against the weight of her natural inclinations. She is ". . . a woman damned to all eternity." [57] Thérèse Desqueyroux, disturbed and unhappy in her marriage, with a positive hate for her husband already beginning to voice itself, wonders what effect her state of mind will have on her unborn child—"What passions might not force an entry into the still unformed flesh within her womb!"[58] Bob Lagave, in particular, is the plaything of his inherited instincts: "Long before he knew what is called evil, so many voices had called to him and tempted him. His ignorant body had been the center of an eddy of appetites and desires. Since his childhood, he had been hemmed in by a silent atmosphere of lust. It was not he who had chosen this path or that; others had chosen for him— poor little Hop-o-my-thumb lost in the ogre's forest. That delicate face of his had been his damnation." [59] Hervé de Blénauge comforts himself with the thought ". . . that he was not alone responsible for whatever was tainted in his own blood. The stream had been already polluted before even he was born." [60] Gabriel Gradère argues ". . . that it is impossible to account for human degradation by the accidents of one poor devil's temperament; that only a downward movement starting from far back can have set going in him the rhythm of deterioration." Gradère, to be sure, is consciously seeking a justification of his own moral lapses. But the abbé Forcas whose besetting temptation has been to brood on "the mystery of evil" is deeply perturbed by Gradère's account of an old priest's declaration that some souls have been given to Satan. The abbé, of course, does not accept the dictum for ". . . if that were so, then all souls must be in like predicament, because, ever since the Fall, each generation of men had inherited from their forebears enough of evil to ensure their damnation . . ." [61] In *The Unknown Sea,* in a passage devoted to the presentation of the perturbation of Pierrot Costadot on his learning of the death of Landin, is a startling comment unquestionably, it would seem from the context, the novelist's own: "The unquenchable fires of hell are lit in *this* world, and those whom theologians count as lost are marked for damnation at their birth, and even before it." [62]

Side by side with these evidences of the physical fatality of human life should be noted Mauriac's tendency to resort, on occasion, to the intervention of an external power or powers to determine man's destiny. Fabien

Dézaymeries arrives in Italy with his awakened senses struggling for liberation from the bonds imposed by an arid and superficial religious practice. His future is fixed by his decision to go to Venice, where he will meet Fanny Barrett, rather than to Rome. Why did he choose Venice? Evidently the decision is made for him—"Not chance, he thought, decides these things." [63] In *Destinies,* Mauriac insists, "Human creatures do not change, but many live along while without knowing themselves, many, indeed, die without doing so—because God has not suffered the evil seed within them to grow, because He may draw towards Himself that frenzy that in some one of their forbears was criminal, and may become so once more in their sons." [64] In *Vipers' Tangle* the aged protagonist who had tirelessly ". . . sought to lose that key which some mysterious hand always gave back . . ." [65] knows it is because his daughter Marie had died for him that he cannot escape regeneration. In *Woman of the Pharisees* Mauriac contrasts the adolescent lovers. Michèle ". . . was one of those human beings whose temperaments are so surely balanced, their hearts so pure, that their instincts are almost always at one with their duty, so that their natural inclinations lead them to do precisely what God expects of them." [66] Jean de Mirbel, on the contrary, ". . . wholly dominated . . . by the blind and irresistible cravings of his senses," and having no one to give him a helping hand, was ". . . the victim of some mysterious fate which seemed to hang over his future. . . ." [67] Among non-fictional characters, Jacqueline Pascal is saved from the temptations of a corrupt court only because it had pleased God to preserve her from that troubled atmosphere, [68] and the life of St. Margaret of Cortona teaches that at the depth of wretchedness a creature may be already elected. [69]

Still, despite apparently emphatic evidence to the contrary, there seems never to have been any real question of Mauriac's formal belief in man's freedom, a freedom confirmed by Grace. As early as *La Vie de Jean Racine* he declares that the human being weaves his destiny out of his own substance. All man's friendships, all his loves carry the stamp of his being. Very few events in human life are unpredictable, the subject almost always setting them in motion. Man's manner of reaction to such happenings as do not proceed from himself is an expression of character. In this reaction he shapes his history. One force alone disturbs the fall of the cards, arresting the natural fatality to introduce a new fatality. It is Christianity. [70] The destiny of Racine was created in the image of his character but of a character thoroughly impregnated with Christianity, not such as nature conceived it. [71] In *God and Mammon* there is a further statement of the same conviction: "In the same sovereign way with which His incarnation breaks the barriers of history, Jesus Christ can choose the favorable moment to come into our lives and unite Himself with the stream of each particular destiny. He wants to introduce His will into this apparent fatality to destroy its fatality." [72] In his *Discours de réception à l'académie française* Mauriac asserts that unless the writer, convinced of the all-sufficiency of Grace, unleashes it in his drama he will be unable to save his characters from that fatality which has remained unchanged since the first crime and the first love. [73] In the first volume of his *Journal* he notes that the maintenance of man's true freedom depends upon the recognition within himself and the elevation above all other concerns of the soul's immutable hunger for God. This accomplished, all the fatalities of life yield and the passions themselves collaborate in the spiritual triumph. "How true it is that the truth makes us free. The miracle of miracles is that Grace has vanquished Necessity." [74] In the second volume of the *Journal,* he suggests that even in a life disordered and in appearance most lost there exists the possibility of sainthood. [75] In *Saint Margaret of Cortona* he writes: ". . . as much as I love Pascal, I hate in him that gloomy pleasure of being elected, when he feels sure that almost nobody else is. . . . The saints upset the cruel logic of Port Royal: they break up the system; they introduce their charming disorder into the calculations of predestination." [76]

The novels and essays alike reveal that the basic problems which called forth the formally theological *Souffrances et bonheur de chrétien* have continued to exercise Mauriac's mind, and, as in *Souffrances and Bonheur*, the effect is of a reiterated debate with Mauriac now emphasizing the power of the downward thrust of man's fallen nature and now the upward lift of Grace. The debt of Pascal is irrefutable despite the rejection of the ultimate Pascalian rigors. Moreover, it should be evident that the vision of Pascal was not imposed upon an unwilling disciple. Clearly Mauriac found confirmation in Pascal for much that was implicit in his own heart. His appeal as a novelist is not only to those who share his beliefs but to those who, in this as in every generation, recognize the validity of the Pascalian anguish though they may count themselves among the followers of Montaigne.

NOTES

1 Commencements d'une vie, *Oeuvres complètes* (Paris: Artheme Fayard, 1951-) IV, 148; *La Rencontre avec Barrès,* IV, 189. Unless otherwise specified, all references to untranslated works are to this edition. Cf. also, *Women of the Pharisees,* tr. Gerard Hopkins (New York: Henry Holt and Company, 1946), p. 144.

2 *Men I Hold Great,* tr. Elsie Pell (New York: Philosophical Library, 1951), p. 1. Cf. also *passim, The Stumbling Block* (New York: Philosophical Library, 1952).

3 *Ibid.,* p. 2.

4 *Paroles catholiques* (Paris: Librairie Plon, 1954), pp. 12-13.

5 *Blaise Pascal et sa coeur Jacqueline*, VIII, 258.

6 *Paroles catholiques*, p. 29.

7 *Blaise Pascal et sa soeur Jacqueline*, VIII, 257.

8 *Ibid.*, 219-220.

9 *Ibid.*, 259.

10 *La Rencontre avec Barrès*, IV, 189.

11 *Paroles catholiques*, pp. 29-31. Cf. also *Bonheur du chrétien*, VII, 253-254.

12 *Bonheur du chrétien*, VII, 270.

13 *Les Maisons fugitives*, IV, 332.

14 *God and Mammon* (New York: Sheed and Ward, Inc., 1936), pp. 86-87.

15 *Ibid.*, p. 9.

16 *Men I Hold Great*, p. 46.

17 *Le Roman*, VIII, 280-281. Cf. also *Proust's Way*, tr. Elsie Pell (New York: Philosophical Library, 1950), pp. 46-47.

18 VI, 122.

19 *Petits essais de psychologie religieuse*, VIII, 29.

20 *Le Roman*, VIII, 281.

21 *Paroles catholiques*, pp. 44-45.

22 *Ibid.*, p. 39.

23 *Saint Margaret of Cortona*, tr. Bernard Frechtman (New York: Philosophical Library, 1948), p. 102.

24 *God and Mammon*, p. 38.

25 *Ibid.*, pp. 99-100.

26 *Souffrances du pécheur*, VII, 243-244.

27 George Hourdin, *Mauriac romancier chrétien* (Paris: Éditions du temps present, 1945), p. 40.

28 *Mauriac: le roman et la vie* (Paris: Le Portulan, 1946), pp. 170-171.

29 "François Mauriac: Étude de Ramon Fernandez," preface to *Dieu et Mammon* (Paris: Éditions du Capitole, 1929), p. 52.

30 *Ibid.*, p. 46.

31 *Paroles catholiques,* p. 31.

32 *Trois récits,* VI, 128.

33 *Genetrix,* tr. Gerard Hopkins (London: Eyre & Spottis-woode, 1950), p. 180.

34 P. 273. These words are also attributed to Blanche Fron-tenac, *The Frontenac Mystery,* tr. Gerard Hopkins (London: Eyre & Spottiswoode, 1951), p. 139.

35 *Destinies,* tr. Eric Sutton (New York: Covici Friede, 1929), p. 51.

36 *La Province,* IV, 465.

37 *Journal,* XI, 234-235.

38 *La Province,* IV, 463. Cf. also *Bonheur de chrétien,* VII, 268 and *Le Fleuve de feu,* I, 260-261.

39 XI, 89.

40 *Ibid.,* 236.

41 *Ibid.,* 232.

42 *Ibid.,* 89.

43 *Ibid.,* 234-236.

44 *God and Mammon,* pp. 26-27.

45 Published first as *Supplément au "Traité de la Concupis-cence" de Bossuet.* Robert J. North notes (pp. 61-62) that in preparing it for publication as *Souffrances du pécheur,* Mauriac softened considerably his protest against the restrictive claims of Catholicism. *Le Catholicisme dans l'oeuvre de François Mauriac* (Editions du Conquistador, 1950), pp. 61-62.

46 VII, 229.

47 VII, 252.

48 *François Mauriac et le problème du romancier Catholique* (Paris: Editions R. A. Correa, 1933), pp. 67-68.

49 VII, 268.

50 *François Mauriac et le problème du romancier Catholique,* pp. 89-90.

51 *Le Catholicisme dans l'oeuvre de François Mauriac,* pp. 66, 67 ff.

52 P. 87.

53 Cf. Hourdin, p. 75; North, pp. 117-118; Joseph Majault, *Mauriac et l'art du roman* (Paris: Robert Laffont, 1946), pp. 227-228.

54 VII, 240.

55 *God and Mammon,* pp. 92-93.

56 IV, 329-330.

57 *The Desert of Love,* tr. by Gerard Hopkins (New York: Pellegrini and Cudahy, 1951), p. 155.

58 *Thérèse,* tr. by Gerard Hopkins (New York: Henry Holt and Co.), p. 54.

59 *Destinies,* p. 138.

60 *That Which Was Lost,* tr. J. A. F. McEwen (London: Eyre & Spottiswoode, 1930), p. 46.

61 *The Mask of Innocence,* tr. Gerard Hopkins (New York: Farrar, Straus & Young, 1953), pp. 9, 136.

62 Tr. Gerard Hopkins (New York: Henry Holt and Co., 1948), p. 212.

63 *The Enemy,* tr. Gerard Hopkins (New York: Pellegrini and Cudahy, 1952), p. 115.

64 P. 200.

65 Tr. Gerard Hopkins (New York: Sheed & Ward, 1947), p. 275.

66 Tr. Gerard Hopkins (New York: Henry Holt and Co., 1946), p. 162. Interestingly, in *The Lamb* (New York: Farrar, Straus and Cudahy, 1955), a novel devoted to the later life of Michele and Jean, the character of Michele has lost its translucence. For further comment on this novel, see Chapter III.

67 Pp. 191, 28.

68 VIII, 173.

69 *Saint Margaret of Cortona* p. 7.

70 VIII 142-143.

71 VIII, 142.

72 P. 96.

73 VIII, 442.

74 XI, 70.

75 XI 118.

76 P. 86.

Neville Braybrooke

THE SEVENTH SKIN:
THE NOVELS OF FRANCOIS MAURIAC

Above the bedclothes, over the sheets, sometimes men
awakening will stare at their hands in amazement—dead
fish gleaming in the moonlight; and, if it is stormy outside and the wind is howling, sometimes those fish will
seem to twitch as if a fin or flipper moved. But reach for
the nearby lamp, flick it on and such ghostly imaginings
vanish. Like the rest of the body, the hands become taken
for granted: men forget the mystery of their flesh, and
not for one instant when they look at it do they remember
those seven mysterious layers of skin which protect them.
Custom has dulled their eyes to the miracle of consciousness.

François Mauriac, I would submit, might de described
as a novelist of the seventh skin. He is concerned not with
outward appearances, but with the heart; not with neat
artistic designs executed as an end in themselves, but with
words as a means of testifying to the Word. Reality is the
aim of his fiction—a reality whose drama is heightened
because it is played against an eternal background. He
has written a *Life of Jesus* (1937) and knows that only
Jesus, had he so decided, could have written the perfect

From BLACKFRIARS, XXXV (October, 1954), 430-38. Reprinted by permission of the publisher and the author.

novel because, being perfect man, his vision was perfect. Others can only hope to report upon the world as they see it and, being fallen creatures, their vision may be faulty. It is the load that all artists who are Christians must accept and carry on their backs. For as Mauriac comments in the American Collected Edition of his works: 'to write means to serve,' and for a novelist to shirk his vocation as a writer is to renounce a God-given trust. Yet as Mauriac continues: 'I am only too well aware how rash it is to conclude that what seems, on all the evidence, to be our determined destiny, must necessarily be the expression of God's will. A vocation for evil, no less than a vocation for good, may well strike sparks from the young' and so, accepting the load, he diminishes his *apologia* to this: '. . . it may be that I was created and set down in one tiny segment of the Universe at a period when Revolt had become the theme on which most of our distinguished thinkers chose to expend their energies, for the sole purpose of bearing witness to Man's guilt when judged by the infinite innocence of God. . . .' The task, then, that Mauriac set himself as a novelist is clear and, looking back on the practice of his art during the last thirty years, it is perhaps salutary to look at the present: to see what form 'Revolt' has taken.

Mauriac's generation was born under the sign of Proust and Freud, and against their 'Revolt,' by examining characters who held their ideas, he has constantly reacted. This is not to infer that he is a reactionary, since, though as a leader-writer of *Le Figaro* he has shown certain right-wing sympathies, in an age whose chief mark has been conformity he has steadily resisted stereotyping his characters—presenting them instead as men and women endowed with separate souls which are as different one from another as are their hands. Outright neither Freud's psychological findings nor Proust's ideas on time are rejected: rather Mauriac believes in complementing them, in enlarging upon them. At least this is the impression which a reader might take away from the novels had he read them one by one as they have been published over the years: but a reader who comes newly upon them, though he will still remain aware of Mauriac's reaction to 'Revolt' as it manifested itself in the 'twenties, 'thirties and 'forties, is likely to gain another emphasis of his reaction to 'Revolt'. Time has as it were changed the perspective, because today the great criteria in fiction are competence and smoothness. Even with a writer so distinguished in his craftsmanship as William Sansom there is a certain deadness in his work and it is only when he is compared with such a writer as Mauriac that one begins to see what causes that deadness. For the characters in Sansom's *contes,* short stories and novels are wonderfully motivated; the criss-crossing of their lives is masterly—and yet, despite this, their actions never become more than those of dancers trippingly and gracefully following the intricacies of a design laid out on some mosaic. As characters in a dance they lack independence because it would seem their author fears to stab them to the heart lest they should bleed and stain the pattern. It would be unsightly and so, because it would be unsightly, blood and guts (except in American fiction) are left out of account. Everything stops short at the seventh skin because to pierce it might prove unhygienic. In other words, no risks other than technical ones are taken lest ragged edges mar the smoothness or untidiness suggest a lack of competence. To restore to the flesh its mystery and to speak truly of the heart Mauriac has risked everything.

In 1922 Grasset published Mauriac's *conte, The Kiss to the Leper,* in his *Cahiers Verts*: in the same series appeared Louis Hemon's *Maria Chapdelaine* and translations of Logan Pearsall Smith's *Trivia* and George Moore's *Memoirs of My Dead Life.* This was not Mauriac's first book, for he had already brought out two volumes of

poetry (in 1940 he brought out another—*Le Sang d'Atys*)
and had four novels to his credit. But from the critics
point of view, *The Kiss to the Leper* meant Mauriac had
arrived: in the French Press he was compared with
Giraudoux, Larbaud and Paul Morand—and certainly
along with *Thérèse Desqueyroux* (1927) and *The Woman
of the Pharisees* (1941) it is among the three peak points
in his achievement. Of the three it is the shortest, and,
in its story of consummated and unrequited love, it states
themes which echo through the rest of the corpus. Jean
Pelouèyre notes of his future wife that 'there were blackheads on her nostrils', and in *The Unknown Sea* (1939)
Robert looks at his wife and notices 'a few blackheads on
the side of her nose'. These are echoing points of detail
which could be multiplied, and may offend the squeamish
for precisely the same reasons as do blood and guts, since
to be squeamish in such matters is to capitulate to 'niceness' rather than the standards of decency. It is to forget
Bossuet's dictum that 'one must know oneself to the pitch
of being horrified'—a dictum which might well serve as
an epigraph to any study of Mauriac. For as men advance
in knowledge of their hearts, so may they get a piercing
vision of their own guilt as fallen creatures 'when judged
by the infinite innocence of God'. In such a view 'niceness' goes by the board, since it follows that Christ was
not crucified on the Cross to safeguard the standards of
respectability but to save men from their sins: crucifixion
was never a hygienic death, and Christ's death on the
Cross for the novelist who is a Christian must inevitably
provide him with an explanation or give him a hint of that
superintending design in which men move. It becomes in
Newman's terms a case of '*if* there be a God, *since* there
is a God, the human race is implicated in some terrible
aboriginal calamity'. The alternative is 'either there is no
Creator, or this living Society of men is in a true sense
discarded from his presence'. Now Newman's arguments,

powerful as they are, are arguments taken from his *Apologia Pro Vita Sua*: they are not the kind of arguments which can be translated into fiction without appearing dogmatic, and it is interesting to see how Mauriac converts such arguments for his own use in *Thérèse Desqueyroux*.

How humiliating cowardice can be! If that Being really did exist (for a brief moment she saw again that Corpus Christi day of blinding heat, a solitary man bowed beneath a golden cope, the Something that he bore between his hands, his moving lips, his look of suffering)—since He *did* exist, let him prevent the criminal act while there was still time. Or, if it was His will that a poor blind soul should open for itself a way to death, let Him at least with love receive the monster He had made. Therese poured the chloroform into the glass. . . .

But to hark back to *The Kiss of the Leper*: to the themes which echo through the rest of the corpus.

As the title suggests, there is the idea of being a leper, an outcaste: '. . . when he pretended to be asleep she got up and kissed him as he lay in his narrow bed—a kiss like those given to lepers by the saints long ago'. Again, in Thérèse Desqueyroux there occurs this passage: 'She was fated to carry loneliness about with her as a leper carries his scabs. "No one can do anything for me: no one can do anything against me. . ." .' And again in *That Which Was Lost* (1930) there is this sentence: 'Then, turning his eyes from the sight of the dead woman, he wept for himself, like a leper horrorstruck at the sight of his own hands'. In each case the leprosy is metaphorical, but it is intended to suggest a feeling of isolation, a sense of lost innocence—that terrible aboriginal calamity in which the human race is implicated. When Noemi Pelouyère discusses with the doctor her husband's illness, and he talks of him as soil specially prepared for the growth of bacilli, as 'tuberculisible' soil, she watches such technical jargon slip from his tongue and reflects: Were not those lips made for kissing? (This is doubly ironic in the context for earlier in the book Jean has thought: 'And how many times did Barbey d'Aurevilly betray the Son of Man for a kiss?'). In another passage in *The Unknown Sea* the idea of lost innocence is stated in even clearer terms.

Seldom is it given to man to realize the precise day and hour, the exact spot on his journey through life, when one whole part of his being falls away, and his face, till then marked by the soft indefiniteness of childhood, suddenly takes on the rigid structure which it will carry with it to the grave.

Such thoughts as these—and the Mauriac canon is interspersed with them throughout—recall Pascal's *Pensées* (which in the Brunchswig edition Mauriac has always carried about with him) and, if these thoughts do not relate to the heart, then they refer to innocence—and the Mauriac connection is this. As children lose their innocence, so they become more and more a prey to concupiscence. Time and again in the novels one discovers this theme being elaborated, with passion being given its full range because in life everything serves as fuel for passion: abstinence sharpens it, repletion strengthens it, virtue irritates it. But here again the squeamish—though this time for different reasons—are shocked: once more 'niceness' is offended. Yet one may recall Mauriac's own reply to Lefevre when he had suggested that he attached too much importance to the flesh in his novels—a criticism also often made of D. H. Lawrence and against which Mauriac has defended him. In his own case Mauriac replied to Lefevre that because most of his generation and their heirs treated the role of the flesh as any other fact it had lost all dramatic value; it had ceased to have anything mysterious about it. In short, to reach the heart the seventh skin must be pierced.

Among the numerous incisions which Mauriac has made there are a multitude on love: 'Nothing is ever wholly serious for those who are incapable of love', and 'All of us, men and women alike, are tender only when we love; never when we are the object of love'. But there are others which might not have come from the *Discours sur les passions de' l'amour,* but suggest rather Montaigne. This, for example: 'Perhaps we know the woman who does not love us better than any other'. There are, too, the directly religious observations such as 'The relation of priest to layman is never neutral: he either attracts or repels', and the more specifically spiritual: 'None would be blessed had they not been given the power to damn themselves. Perhaps, only those are damned who might have been saints.' In all these instances is reflected that personal impersonality which is the paradox of Pascal and, in *The Frontenac Mystery* (1933), the switch from personal narrative to impersonal statement—yet a statement in which all are implicated—is superbly realized by Mauriac: 'In some obscure region of himself he knew what the future held—for we are always warned'. The thinker and novelist have become one.

None the less not always are the transitions so easy, and the three charges commonly brought that Mauriac is a Jansenist, Manichaean and sensualist all have their grain of truth because there are times when Mauriac steps out of the realms of fiction, buttonholes the reader and tells him what he has personally set out to do. To preface thus *The Knot of Vipers* (1932) amounts to both a form of spiritual and literary cheating.

The man here depicted was the enemy of his own flesh and blood. His heart was eaten up by hatred and avarice. Yet, I would have you, in spite of his baseness, feel pity, and be moved by his predicament. All through his dreary life squalid passions stood between him and the radiance which was so close that an occasional ray could still break through to touch and burn him: not only his own passions, but, primarily, those of the lukewarm Christians who spied upon his actions, and whom he himself tormented. Too many of us are similarly at fault, driving the sinner to despair and blinding his eyes to the light of truth. . . .

Enough! These are the flowery accents of the parochial sermon and in any case their author and his central character the miser are much better served in the quotation from St. Teresa of Avila which preludes the story. '. . . Consider, O God, that we are without understanding of ourselves; that we do not know what we would have, and set ourselves at an infinite distance from our desires'. This is the vein in which Mauriac declared in 1923 that it was his intention 'by presenting creatures entirely deprived of a religious life' to show 'the emptiness of souls —an emptiness especially notable among women'. The statement was without frills, but it was a bold and dangerous undertaking because, in using words to defend the Word and in asserting the mystery of the flesh, it meant presenting men and women who, true to the 'Revolt' of their era in girding against themselves and so become aware of that Divine Image in which they were created. To the Hound of Heaven, had Pascal lived in the nineteenth century, he might have said: 'One always loses the game!' and, had Nietzsche eavesdropped, he might have added: 'One always loses the game—even your brain!' For Nietzsche's retort, had he made it as a final gird against Fate, would have sounded to Mauriac as a cry for Grace, because Mauriac's characters often have many resemblances with Nietzsche. They want to be Masters— Masters of their Fates—and when they fall (so the novelist would suggest) it is because they do not see the tripwires which have been laid by Grace. Sometimes however the wires are seen by the needer and the effect is lost. *The Enemy* (1935) ends: '. . . Grace? It is the mark of our slavery and of our wretchedness that we can, without lying, paint a faithful portrait only of the passions' and immediately the veil of fiction is off: the *conte* appears didactic rather than dramatic and, pithy as such an observation is, it is out of place and would be better relegated to an author's journal. In fact this concluding remark comes as an anti-climax in *The Enemy* and so detracts in the total effect from some of the wires which, earlier and better laid, have done their work in such a natural yet supernatural way that a reader has not stopped to exclaim: 'A trick—a trick device! Spiritual cheating!'; but rather: 'How odd! That's always happening in life!'

An artist who is true to the heart, however religious he may be, cannot rely upon a pietistic *deus ex machina;* nor upon a sudden conversion nor the improbably abandonment of the loose habits of a lifetime. If such changes are to take place they must be psychologically conditioned changes (and in this matter Mauriac has learnt much from Freud), since if they do occur they must have an air of likelihood about them. A formula mechanically employed is worse than useless because it is the artist's function to re-create living experience; and because life today in any large city gives such an emphasis to sex, it is natural that sex will play a large role in any modern novel. To neglect it would be to exchange the real world for the world of swaddling clothes; to see men and women as from the prison of a cot, in which the bars obscure the vision. On the contrary, the artist or novelist who can pierce through to the heart and see life as it is, can also see life *as it could be.* For instance, when Doctor Courreges bends over his adored who is also his patient in *The Desert of Love* (1925) it is as a man of science, not a lover.

Leaning over the naked breast whose veiled loveliness had once made him tremble, he listened to her heart, then, very gently touching her injured forehead with his finger, he traced the extent of the wound. 'Does it hurt you here . . . or here . . . or here?' She complained, too, of pain on her lip. Very carefully he drew down the sheet so as to expose no more than the small bruised surface; then covered it up again. With his eyes on the watch, he felt her pulse. The body had been delivered to him for cure, not possession. His eyes knew that they were there to observe, not to be enchanted. He gazed intently at her flesh, bringing all his intelligence to bear. The clearness of his mind barred all roads of approach to his melancholy passion. . . .

For the duration of this medical visit concupiscence remains a dead thing and it is a tribute to Mauriac's craftsmanship that he is able to induce a similar feeling in the reader—though it is an even greater tribute to his mastery of style and technique that his writing in this chapter is so taut that it carries along with it a number of corollaries that automatically flow out of the scene. One is made aware of something more than Doctor Courrege's purely scientific approach to Maria Cross' body. One is made aware of modesty itself; of that unfathomable *sapientia* in which love is locked away and wherein resides the mystery of woman. For love alone may strip itself bare and any other nakedness must perforce be a betrayal: to accept this is to assign to the flesh its true importance and sanctity, because when love is betrayed each betrayal is a further emptying of the soul, a further loss of innocence. As Mauriac himself has noted as a novelist: 'you become less pure' and, though concupiscence and its effects have taken most of his attention, there is also the theme of spiritual pride which is the controllng theme in *The Woman of the Pharisees*—a hint of which was given a decade previously in *That Which Was Lost*. 'Irene had always had an idea that by the mere fact of visiting the poor and ministering to their wants she somehow justified the existence of poverty.' Brigitte Pian has the same idea, but, hypocrite as she is, there are moments when her defenses are down—moments when she reveals herself as a woman of the Pharisees and at the same time, because she is not a stock character, shows that is within her one day to know herself to the pitch of being horrified. She remains continually a potential saint—the potentiality of which suddenly becomes apparent to the reader during an outburst. 'You know very well that it will be so because it is my will . . . she checks herself. And when I say "my will", I express myself badly, for we must not do what we will, but what God wills. . . . ' The point is made perfectly: this may be the first twinge of conscience, the beginning of a return to innocence, but innocence the wiser for experience. For there is a scene in this book between the subsidiary characters which clinches the relationship of innocence to experience. Here is the paragraph in question:

The two young people who had fallen in love before the lines of their physical development had become fully determined, looked at one another with astonishment. There was what seemed to me a long interval of silence. The poor human insects had to trace backwards the stages of their metamorphosis before each could see once more in the other the child whom he and she had loved. But their eyes had not changed, and it was they, I am sure, which first gave them the clue to their identities.

The paragraph is characteristic. The telling phrase 'the poor human insects' recalls Pascal's comparison between man and God, an insect and man. For if Mauriac's picture of men without God is set in the Landes country where pine trees stretch out endlessly and the fear of fire is perpetual, where sheep in winter are the color of dead ash and where every sort of scheming known in bourgeois circles is practiced to keep plate and linen in the same family, where ten years' habitat in Paris makes a man no more than a provincial abroad—if these and a thousand other details may localize the Mauriac landscape they do not detract from its universal significance. As the ways of God seem inscrutable to men, so too, perhaps, *le coeur a ses raisons que la raison connoit pas.*

Sister Anita Marie Caspary, I.H.M.

THE THEME OF ISOLATION IN
MAURIAC'S *THE DESERT OF LOVE*

"The Desert of Love might well serve as the title for my entire work."

Mauriac in "My Novels,"
Commonweal [1]

A theme pervading many of the novels of Mauriac and providing a key to his view of human life and love is the concept of the essential isolation of each human being. That loneliness, that natural "impenetrability of souls," according to Fernandez [2] always marks the dramatic conflicts of the novels of Mauriac. Jacques Robichon writes, "Cette solitude de l'homme au milieu de ses semblables, Mauriac l'a explorée; il est allé jusqu'à la définir." [3]

To suggest, however, that Mauriac's treatment of isolation is comparable to the existentialist concern with "estrangement" would be thoroughly to misunderstand him. [4] For Mauriac, the isolation of the human person most frequently parallels his conviction of the futility of human love in attempting to possess another. But this dual theme is a distortion unless it is seen as supplementary to the

From TWENTIETH CENTURY LITERATURE, VII, No. 3 (October 1961), 107-113. Reprinted by permission of the publisher, Alan Swallow.

thesis, central to Mauriac, that love of God alone can truly penetrate the "secret city" [5] of the human heart. To trace the theme of human isolation and its relative position in Mauriac's writing is, therefore, highly significant in the study of his thought.

In the Mauriac canon, the themes of isolation, the frustration of human love in attempting communion with another, and the ultimate confrontation with the "Other" are recurrent with variations of every kind. Thus the desperate attempt of passion to shatter the isolation of another human heart is described in a vivid passage in *The River of Fire,* sequel to *The Desert of Love.* The use of the first person plural implies philosophical universality of experience:

We may for days have longed to clasp another human body. The point has come when we can persuade ourselves that we have possession within our grasp. We hug and hold the prey within our arms. We burn in the furnace of our blood. Sensual magic has wrought a transference, so that we see with our hands, touch with our eyes. All resistance has ceased: at last, surrender is complete. We enter the very being of the prize. We draw in the very breath of its life, but even then we do not possess it. Our furious tide beats against another's being, dashes against a living wall, bursts through, ebbs back, but never finds the ultimate satisfaction. . . . The ingenuities of lust are powerless. By the ways of the flesh we try to achieve the mastery of another's being. But we never do. [6]

The notion that human love is a betrayal, that the creatures we think we love do not actually exist at all but are merely reflections of ourselves whom we seek in the blind desire for union with the "Other" is the theme of *The Loved and the Unloved.* In the book, Nicolas Plassac is pursued, as Mauriac himself tells us, by a woman convinced that, "even in love, the force of sheer determination, of sheer will-power, can be made to triumph." [7] But in the last lines, Nicolas, now freed both of this woman and his sentimental friendship with Gilles Salone, is thus described:

He started to walk again and reached the place where the road crossed the Leyrot. He sat upon the parapet, a stranger to himself, detached from all his fellows. It was as though he had agreed with somebody to meet him there. [8]

On this passage Mauriac enlarged in the *Postscript* to comment:

. . . that "someone" waiting for Nicolas Plassac where the road crosses the Leyrot *is* God. But before that meeting could take place I had first to destroy the idol—Gilles Salone. It was necessary that Nicolas should be detached from appearances, from his own false image of himself. [9]

Further commentary of Mauriac on the illusion of union with another in human love is found in *The Stumbling Block* where he quotes first of all his heroine of *The End of the Night*, Therese Descroyoux:

Life with the creature we love should be a long siesta in the sun, a repose without end, an animal quietude: the certainty that someone is there, within reach of our hand, in harmony with us, amenable, fulfilled to overflowing; and that he could not want, any more than we do, to be anywhere else. Round about, there should be such a torpor that even thought is engulfed, that there may be no possibility of betrayal, even in the mind . . . [10]

But again, on this passage Mauriac adds:

The desire for caresses and for human warmth still finds expression here, but there are already indications, preparations for another state in which the creature imperceptibly withdraws, is no longer inside us but at our side, until at last the Other approaches. [11]

In one of Mauriac's later novels, *The Lamb*, there is the startling description of the hero, Xavier Dartigelogue, in an image reminiscent of *The Desert of Love;* Xavier is seen battling against the "temptation of others" which diverts him from the total dedication to God he desires:

Each time that he knew for certain that somebody had landed on his island, penetrated into his desert, then he must flee from him; for that desert was his portion in the world, his cross. Not to feel that he was alone would mean that he had come down from his cross. [12]

Perhaps the best material for the analysis of Mauriac's treatment of human isolation is found in the novel *The Desert of Love* in which, as Michael F. Moloney puts it, "incommunicability is particularly evident." [13] In this novel, the theme that God alone will satisfy the human heart is fundamental and is found in the structure of incidents as well as in the commentary of the basic voice.

The Desert of Love opens with the meeting, after seventeen years, of Raymond Courreges, a burned out roué of thirty-five, and Maria Cross, the now fortyish woman who initiated his career by her scorn of him. As a spoiled, indolent widow of twenty-seven, Maria, mistress of the wealthy Victor Larousselle, had deliberately attracted her physician, Dr. Courreges. Tiring of him, she then pursues Raymond, his grubby, adolescent son. Flattered by her attentions and her half-serious show of affection, Raymond makes passionate advances toward Maria who, disgusted and sickened by his youthful brutality, repels him. Maria, frightened and ashamed by the episode, comes face to face with herself and her pathetic, restless quest for love, but Raymond's frustration vents itself in a life of revenge on women.

This encounter in a Paris bar after many years, brings Raymond the realization that Maria has chosen a life of self-sacrifice by her marriage to Larousselle, giving respectability to a stepson whom she obviously worships as a saint. Raymond is nonplussed by the Maria of the present whose recollection of their past "affair" seems dim and unreal. Dr. Courreges, called in to attend the drunken Larousselle, also finds Maria still lovely but completely indifferent. The trio who had caused each other such pain meet for a few moments over Larousselle's semi-conscious form. Maria's fearful quest for identity and security has ended in finding God, or at least in serving someone beyond herself. For the Courreges, father and son, the future is still tragic:

There could be no hope for either of them, for father or for son, unless, before they died, He should reveal Himself, who, unknown to them, had drawn and summoned from the depths of their beings this burning bitter tide. [14]

The theme of human isolation is used as counterpoint against this structure of incidents. Recognition of their impenetrability and solitude as individuals is found in the thoughts of Maria, of Raymond, and of Doctor Courreges, suggesting that neither age, nor sex, nor personality changes this basic trait of human nature. After the episode in which Raymond attempts to attack Maria, she reflects:

Is not my lot, thought Maria, the common lot of all womankind? Without husband, without children, no one, indeed, could be more lonely than herself. But was this solitude more actual or more intense than the sense of isolation from which no family life, however happy, could have saved her—the sense of being alone which comes to all of us as soon as we learn to recognize in ourselves the distinguishing marks of that accursed species, the race of lost souls whose instincts, needs, and mysterious ends we alone can interpret? [15]

Here the reflection proceeds strikingly from the unique situation of the individual to an implied universal statement emphasized by the author's skillful change to first person plural.

The theme of human isolation is again found in the soliloquy of Doctor Courreges. Considering his hopeless love for Maria Cross, the doctor concludes that his own isolation is inescapable:

It was the law of his nature that he could never make contact with those he loved. He had never been more conscious of that truth than in those moments of partial success when he had held in his arms the object so long desired, and found it suddenly poor and dwarfed and utterly different from what it had been in the agonies of his desire. No reason to seek in the mirror the reasons for that solitude in which he was fated to remain until his death. . . . But he, even in his youth, had been obedient only to the call of his pre-destined solitude. (p. 163)

The possible implication in the above passage that the realization of isolation may be confined to the meditative man, the intellectual, as opposed to Raymond, the more aggressive man, the extrovert, is denied later in the book. In the final pages of *The Desert of Love* Mauriac writes of Raymond:

On the brink of this appalling emptiness, of this day without Maria, which was to be but the first of many days without her, he was made aware, at one and the same moment, of his dependence and his solitude. (p. 212)

Thus by means of the author's commentary or through the reflections of the individual characters, Maria, Doctor Courreges, and Raymond are all seen to be conscious of their own isolation.

While the theme of isolation in *The Desert of Love* is thus stated in passages of reflection throughout the novel, it is chiefly through his patterns of imagery that Mauriac touches on this theme and places it in its subordinate and supporting position. The title of the novel, in its use of the image "Le desert," gives, according to Jacques Robichon, the image central to all of Mauriac's thinking on the problem of human solitude. [16] Mauriac says of himself: "The Desert of Love! I was born with the knowledge of this desert." [17]

Love, in the experience of Maria Cross, Raymond Courreges, and his father, Doctor Courreges, is a barren thing; it is a desert with all of the accompanying connotations. Love for this trio is a place of solitude and utter desolation, a place of temporary oasis which eventually and inevitably becomes a mirage. It is a place where one may become dessicated and devitalized as does Doctor Courreges, maddened in the heat of passion as does Raymond, or brought to one's knees as is Maria Cross in the loneliness where only God and oneself exist.

The desert image is found early in the text itself where Mauriac describes Raymond as a painfully self-conscious adolescent finding temporary relief from his isolation in the "shared immersion of a trolley car driving through the suburban night." (p. 52) Mauriac writes of Raymond:

It never occurred to him that one spoken word would have been enough to conjure up the desert that separates classes as surely from one another as it does individuals. (p. 52)

Mauriac employs the desert image next in describing the impotence of human love in breaking the isolation of the individual:

The doctor loved Maria, but he could see her with detachment. He loved her as the dead must love the living. . . . No more successfully at twenty-five than now could he have crossed the desert separating this woman and himself. . . . It was the law of his nature that he could never make contact with those he loved. (pp. 162-163)

The desert image is found again in a passage of reflection to convey the concepts both of isolation and of spiritual aridity when Maria despairs of a return visit from Raymond, her young admirer:

Maria Cross had filled up the last well to be found in her desert. Nothing now but sand. The most dangerous of all things in love is the flight of one of the parties to the plot. (p. 141)

The desert image is used finally of Maria in combination with another image of isolation, that of the planet. More complex in its philosophical implications than Mauriac's previous use of the desert image, this passage conveys in Maria's feeling the human desire for self-surrender. The notion of self-containment is meanwhile suggested by the planet image while the term "desert" retains the connotation of fruitlessness. The passage comes at the end of the attempted attack by Raymond; it is Maria's "moment of illumination:"

Leaning out into the night air, drawn, almost physically absorbed, by the quietness of the vegetable world, Maria Cross yielded not so much to a desire to drink deep of the branch-encumbered air as to a temptation to lose herself in it, to feel herself dissolved and atomized, till the inner desert of her heart should become one with the emptiness of space, till the silence within her should in no way differ from the silence of the spheres. (p. 158)

The concept of the sphere, the planet, visualized as a microcosm self-contained and associated with other bodies in a gigantic but uncommunicative system, is Mauriac's most frequently chosen image of isolation in *The Desert of Love*. In his first use of this image, Mauriac shows not two heavenly bodies but rather the earthly observer and the untouchable planet he watches. Raymond is described as isolated by lack of communication from the woman Maria, as they ride in the trolley:

He, too, feeling safe because he had nothing to fear from this stranger, not even a word, since nothing had built a bridge between them, stared back with that tranquil intensity with which we gaze upon a distant planet. (p. 54)

The psychological impact of this image is peculiarly effective, since the watcher, Raymond, and the planet, Maria, are both pictured as serenely undisturbed by each other's presence or gaze, in contradistinction to the cataclysms which each will soon cause the other. At the same time, the distance and ethereal beauty of the planet as contrasted with the earthly viewer suggest the distinctive loveliness of Maria as opposed to the uncouth adolescent who stares at her.

74

The notion of different peoples inhabiting different planets implies in each group a vague knowledge of each other's existence, but there is complete disparity of atmosphere and great difficulty in communication; in any case, the attempt to reach each other seems somewhat futile. This image describes the doctor and his mother:

One can tell nothing unless one tells all. How could he expect this old lady to understand the music that sounded so deep in her son's heart, with its lacerating discords? He was of another race than hers, being of another sex. They were separated more surely than people living on two different planets. (p. 57)

The Desert of Love furnishes several unique and striking images of isolation where a human being is seen in an atmosphere not properly his own from which he must escape at the peril of his life. The images thus freighted with emotional power are those of the prisoner, the miner, and the diver. The image of the prisoner is curiously revealing, for it operates in reverse. The picture is that of Doctor Courreges:

He was done with suffering, with beating, like a prisoner, against the walls of his cell. The vital force which had been his since childhood, but which the pressure of so many human creatures had led him to dissipate, he now took back, thrusting it deep, deep into himself. (p. 88-89)

The image of the miner is used of Dr. Courreges and his wife to describe the special isolation in which others enclose us by their misunderstanding and the extinction of personality to which this enforced estrangement condemns us:

From somewhere beyond the wretched fabric of words that she had built up, from somewhere beyond the wall that her vulgarity had erected, with antlike patience, day by day, Lucie Courreges could hear the stifled cry of a man who was buried alive, the shout of an imprisoned miner, and deep within herself, too, another voice replied to his . . . (p. 94)

A peculiarly powerful image is that of the diver. Mauriac uses it to describe Raymond, who has lived since adolescence in this sea-atmosphere of remembered passion for Maria:

What passion might occupy her mind he could not know. She was armed against him, separated from him, by the accumulated experiences of seventeen years. Like a dazed and blinded diver he fought his way to the surface, up from the dead past. (pp. 180-181)

In *The Desert of Love,* Mauriac draws the major theme —that Divine Love is man's only fulfillment—in bold outline. As this brief survey suggests, to describe the various aspects of human isolation as a secondary theme he employs chiefly a wide range of imagery. By his skill in the use of this technique, Mauriac implies delicately but unmistakeably that human isolation is viewed by him only against the background of God's ability to satisfy the lonely human heart.

NOTES

1 Vol. LVIII, No. 6 (May 15, 1953), p. 142.
2 "Francois Mauriac: Etude de Ramon Fernandez," Preface to *Dieu et Mammon* (Paris: Editions du Capitole, 1929), p. 54.
3 *Francois Mauriac* (Paris: Editions Universitaires, c. 1953), p. 9.
4 This theme of isolation or "estrangement" is easily traced in contemporary literature, particularly that written under the aegis of existentialism. Dr. Kurt F. Reinhardt, discussing this theme in *The Existentialist Revolt* (Milwaukee, 1952), shows how the feeling of man as stranger, "locked out and alone within himself" pervades the poetic work of Rilke, in such a poem as *The Great Night*. Man as "stranger to the world into which he has been 'thrown' and in which he is inescapably involved" is the motif in Kafka's *The Trial* and *The Castle*. And Sartre's world is

"populated by contingent and isolated beings, all self-enclosed and merely physically juxtaposed in a metaphysical and moral vacuum," as is seen in *Huis-clos* and *Les Mouches.* (pp. 232 ff.)

5 *Woman of the Pharisees,* trans. Gerard Hopkins (New York, 1948) p. 125.

6 *The River of Fire,* trans. Gerard Hopkins (London, 1954), pp. 96-97.

7 *The River of Fire,* pp. 62-63.

8 *The Loved and the Unloved,* trans. Gerard Hopkins (New York, 1952), p. 148.

9 *The Loved and the Unloved,* p. 143.

10 *The Loved and the Unloved,* pp. 146-147.

11 Pp. 52-53.

12 *The Stumbling Block* (New York, 1952), p. 53.

13 *The Lamb,* trans. Gerard Hopkins (New York, 1954), p. 28.

14 *Francois Mauriac* (Denver, 1958), p. 106.

15 *The Desert of Love* (New York, 1951), p. 158. All quotations from *The Desert of Love* are taken from the edition translated by Gerard Hopkins and published by Pellegrini & Cudahy in 1951.

16 *Francois Mauriac,* p. 9 and pp. 40 ff.

17 Quoted by Elsie Pell in *Francois Mauriac: In Search of the Infinite* (New York, 1947), p. 36.

James Finn

MAURIAC

"As a man grows older he becomes more conscious of eternal things. He becomes less restive, so that the voices coming from beyond can be heard more clearly. As eternity closes in, the reality of time begins to fade."

Do these words of Romano Guardini, which Francois Mauriac quoted approvingly more than ten years ago, apply to Mauriac himself? Has the highly restive spirit which over the years Mauriac has so generously disclosed in poems, novels, plays, journals, criticism, biography, polemics, religious essays, political journalism—has that spirit, the cause of whose restlessness he once so eloquently debated with Gide, become at last relaxed and restful? Do we find in his most recent book, *What I Believe,* a disconcertingly unfamiliar figure?

The answer to these questions must be "No." The purpose of this book, according to Mauriac, is to answer the question, "Why have you remained faithful to the religion into which you were born?" The question itself is very familiar to his readers, as is the kind of response he makes, a response which hinges on the personal, concrete details of his life and his reading. (And how familiar, too, to his readers must be that Braunschvig edition of Pascal's *Pensées* which Mauriac first owned when he was

From JUBILEE, 11 (February 1964), 45-51. Reprinted by permission of the publisher.

sixteen.) In *What I Believe* Mauriac attempts once again to strip back another layer of his personality, to throw more light on the hidden recesses of his nature, to approach even more closely the very impulse of his being. There are, admittedly, some differences from his earlier attempts at the same task if for no other reason than that the history of a man of 76 is different from that of a man of thirty, forty or even sixty. But the poles around which Mauriac's thought has constantly turned, those steadfast magnets of his spirit, those springs of his passion were established long ago in Bordeaux, where the hothouse atmosphere of his religious schooling and the firm religious practices of a fond mother made only more acute his response to the complacent, hypocritical bourgeoisie who were his friends and neighbors.

In *Commencements d'une Vie,* a proposed autobiography which proved so painful that he completed only a few pages, Mauriac wrote, "The history of Bordeaux is the history of my body and my soul." Although he left Bordeaux for Paris when he was twenty, it is there that his themes were given him. It is on the narrow provincial life of his childhood that he focuses his own narrow, intense vision, and the very souls of his characters correspond to the contours of the Bordeaux landscape. Through that landscape of sandy coastal plains stunned by the sun, of drowsing vines and cool winestores, of pine forests moaning in the breeze or bursting into flame, run streams of lust and loneliness, of avarice and jealousy. In this landscape Cybele opposes her claims to those of Christ, rival claims whose clash Mauriac has recounted over the years. Who could distinguish readily among the following sentiments:

Christianity makes no provision for the flesh. It suppresses it.

In a young man, the hidden powers of the flesh and the demands of reason are conjugated against Christ.

The Church does not trust the flesh because she knows the flesh fell with Adam.

I knew that the Christian God demanded everything. I knew that He had no part in the flesh and that the world of nature and the world of grace were two and inimical.

The fourth statement was made in an address he delivered in 1929, the second in this book he wrote last year, and the others at various years in between. Yet the accent is unvarying, the tensions constant. They are those which, pressed into the service of his imaginative works, very soon brought the young Mauriac the admiration and critical approval of important literary elders and the disapprobation and suspicion of many of his fellow Catholics.

In *Maria Cross,* a valuable study of a group of modern Catholic writers, Conor Cruise O'Brien offers the comment of a critic whose opinions presumably formed those of all proper French families in the twenties, Abbé Louis Bethléem. In 1928, after Mauriac had produced what must still rank among his best work, the Abbé described him as "A rural author, subject to the intoxication of the fields and initiated into the frivolities of Parisian life." Most of Mauriac's works were readily summed up.

Le Fleuve de feu: disturbing, unhealthy

Génitrix: bizarre, morbid

Le Desert de l'amour: very pernicious

Thérèse Desqueyroux: morally unhealthy

These opinions were shared by many other prominent Catholic critics and O'Brien quotes an authority superior to the Abbé (Père Eugène Charles), who said that Mauriac's novels were "steeped in an atmosphere of refined sensuality which penetrates to the marrow of your bones."

Whatever the literary merit of these judgments they are unwilling testimony to the power of Mauriac's dark imagination. Mauriac has frequently expressed bewilderment that his books should be thought somber when, he points out, they are shot through with the mysterious workings of grace. But even a brief consideration of a couple of his best works will make clear the basis of this description.

Génitrix opens with Fernand Cazenave and his mother standing at the bedside of his wife, Mathilde, as she, pretending to sleep, watches on the wall their large, overlapping shadows. As they move away, Mathilde, who is dying of deliberate neglect in this bleak room at some remove from the center of the house, reviews her small life. Brought up in poverty, she married an older man who saw the marriage as an escape from the domination of his mother. But he was as unable to free himself from his mother's overbearing authority as he was incapable of bringing any joy into Mathilde's life. And the baby which might have shifted the balance was stillborn. Now this body of Mathilde's "was going to be consumed in death that had never been consumed in love. No annihilation in caresses had prepared it for the eternal dissolution."

Mathilde's death leaves Mme. Felicité triumphant, for her son is once again undeniably, unreservedly hers. But no, Fernand finds it easier to develop some feeling for the memory of his wife than he ever did for her. Her absence becomes an ever increasing barrier between mother and son, who live now in a suffocating, enclosed atmosphere in which it seems impossible for life to sustain itself. Mme. Cazenave dies, estranged from the only love her life has known.

Fernand's spiritual solitude now finds its counterpart in his physical isolation. An aged servant is his only possible human contact and the novel ends with his acknowledgment that he needs her comfort.

Many Mauriacean virtues are developed to a highly refined point in this novel. Its sparse, unadorned structure, its unrelieved, harsh beauty, its concentration on a few characters, its depth of psychological penetration, its absolute authority of style and tone—all these unite to make *Génitrix* a peak of Mauriac's achievement.

In *Génitrix* Mauriac has chosen to show not the attraction of the flesh, the feverish reaching out of lover to loved, for which he is noted, but to reveal the aridity of life where no such love breaks in, that solitude which can be breached—if only momentarily—by some shattering love. He does suggest, however, that even the oppressive care Felicité imposed on her son may have been born of a distorted love: "Perhaps there is only one love."

Mauriac has said that *The Desert of Love* might serve as the title of his entire work, and most readers would agree. Yet this novel differs from *Génitrix* in several important ways. It is longer, it has more scope, it develops not straightforwardly but with an intricate shifting of time and place, it mingles several important themes and it presents characters who are each of equal importance.

"For years Raymond Courrèges had been cherishing the hope that one day he might encounter Maria Cross, the woman upon whom he so ardently longed to be revenged." Sitting in a bar in Paris he does unexpectedly see her, and his mind is thrown back to that brief period seventeen years earlier when he, a schoolboy of eighteen, crossed the path of a worldly woman of twenty-seven. And from his recollections, weaving back and forth through time, we learn of those events so decisive in his life: Raymond himself is a grubby, solitary schoolboy whose thoughts turn readily to sex; Maria Cross is a neighborhood scandal, the mistress of a wealthy wine merchant, the mother of a recently buried child, a relatively passive, sentimental woman.

But when they see each other on the trolley that takes him back from school and Maria back from the cemetery, he appears to her romantic eyes a "sullen angel," a picture of what her son might have been, a dream of pure innocence. And Raymond gradually comes to see her as a wonderfully available incarnation of his fevered dreams. Although it is January when they first see each other, "there was already in the foggy air the secret sweetness of the coming season."

The illusions each has about the other lead to a terrible scene in which Raymond, attempting to force himself upon her, is repelled and mocked. From that moment on Raymond determined—and successfully—to take his revenge on every woman he met, waiting always for that sweetest revenge on Maria. Maria, repelled in turn by her own fanciful notions about Raymond, attempts suicide.

These events, both in actuality and in narration, are interwoven with the activities of Raymond's father, Dr. Courrèges. For it is this shy, lonely, successful doctor who has treated her child, sympathized with her position and attempted vainly to communicate his love for her. But Maria, seeing in the doctor only an admirable old bore, remains unaware of his feeling.

These form the main elements of the story which is resolved in the final pages when these three pilgrims of a single absolute are brought together once again around the sickbed of the wine merchant, whom Maria had finally married.

This summary of events brutalizes the most subtle, complex relations which exist between these characters and their understanding of each other, omits completely that poetic quality which is Mauriac's singular strength, gives no hint of the distorting constrictions of the provincial life, and fails even to suggest the power with which Mauriac evokes those adolescent years when, for some, the hot needle-flow of blood pulses along the veins and allows no respite to the imagination. What the summary does do is reveal those themes to which Mauriac obsessively returns: the loneliness and solitude which is, for him, each man's fate, try as one will to oppose it; the fateful attractions of the flesh which promise more than they can offer ("To possess the body of another is to embrace a corpse"); the constant pull of that one love for which we attempt fleeting substitutes ("Not loves but only one love in us," says Maria); the sweetness of youth and the ravages of age ("At twenty-three he was already suffering: ever since his eighteenth year he had been agonizingly aware that he was growing older").

Mauriac was forty when he wrote *The Desert of Love; What I Believe* reaffirms what he has elsewhere disclosed, that he then entered upon an extremely troubled period of his life. "For two or three years, it seemed as if I had lost my mind. Almost nothing of this was visible on the outside. The episodic reasons for this madness concealed more obscure reasons coming from the intersection of the flesh and the soul at that midway point in life when a man enters the forties. . . . I have often thought that You were never closer to me than during those days of endless suffering when I could easily at any moment have plunged into death. I wandered about Paris like a lost dog, like a collarless dog."

Aside from Mauriac's own preoccupation with age, several other events concurred to trouble his mind at this time. For while his novels brought him the acclaim and assurance he had sought, they also brought charges that he was putting his religion in the service of sensual attraction, charges to which at this point he became extremely sensitive. He wrote in these years 1928-1929 several essays which have caused some critics to dramatize this period as a time of "conversion" for Mauriac. *Souffrances du chrétien* is an anguished cry in which, as he later said, he attempted "to persuade people that my religion was both true and impracticable—so as to excuse my own powerlessness to conform my life to it." Six months later appeared *Bonheur du chrétien,* a "recantation" in which he wrote that "the Author of life takes vengeance by so overwhelming this soul and this body in His love that he confesses the law of the spirit to be, indeed, the law of the flesh." He also wrote at this time *God and Mammon,* his brilliant response to Andre Gide who had written to him a letter which charged that "what you are searching for is the *permission* to write *Destins*—the permission to be a Catholic without having to burn your books; and it is this that makes you write them in such a way that you will not have to disown them on account of your Catholicism. This [is a] reassuring compromise, which allows you to love God without losing sight of Mammon. . . . Doubtless if I were more of a Christian I should be less your disciple."

In *God and Mammon* there are examined with nonsystematic subtlety and eloquence the profound and ever-recurrent problems of literature and morality, the responsibility of the artist, and—as always for Mauriac—the rival clams of Cybele and Christ, of human love and divine. And Mauriac, who also responded to Maritain's strictures in those pages, had a right to be satisfied with his analyses of his position.

Mauriac's passage through these troubled years was safe if perilous. But it did not bring him into some calm, untroubled harbor. Among the many novels he wrote after this, three especially are worth special attention: *The Vipers' Tangle* because it has claim to being classed with his best work and is a strong argument against the theory of Mauriac's artistic conversion; *Le fin de la nuit* because it came under notable attack; and *Woman of the Pharisees* because of its merits, however uneven, and because it is a partial answer to the attack.

Mauriac survived the charges of being a novelist who was not sufficiently Christian to run into the charge that he was a Christian but no novelist. In 1939, Jean Paul

Sartre, who was not then well known, wrote in *Nouvelle Revue Française,* a devastating attack on Mauriac. Selecting *Le fin de la nuit* because it deals with the problem of freedom, Sartre dissected it mercilessly, exposing real flaws. He ended his essay by saying that Mauriac had "chosen divine omniscience and omnipotence. But novels are written *by* men and *for* men. In the eyes of God, Who cuts through appearance and goes beyond, there is no novel, no art, for art thrives on appearances. God is not an artist. Neither is M. Mauriac."

For many younger readers this essay sapped the foundations of a fixture who had been around for many years, a failing novelist whose fogeyism had been certified years earlier by his membership in *l'Academie Française.* Of the half dozen novels Mauriac has written since that essay, *Woman of the Pharisees* is the clearest artistic response to Sartre, whose attack he had in mind when he wrote it. While it is the best of his later fictions it does not reach the heights of his earlier works.

In addition to more than twenty novels and some short stories, Mauriac has written four plays, two of which are important; a life of Racine which, in addition to its intrinsic merit, discloses his affinity with a writer he much admired; a life of Jesus, which Henri de Lubac classed with those of Dickens and Papini, not meaning any compliment; four volumes of verse; and, in late years, much political journalism.

His columns in the liberal *L'Express* have, in fact, gained for him renewed fame and notoriety. Those on the Right have dismissed these columns as the work of a vain old man declining into senility, as the expected continuation of his familiar assault on the bourgeoisie, as the ravings of a man blinded by political partisanship. But the intensity of their response is the best indication that many of his shafts have gone home. What causes his opponents to rage at him is not his particular political position, not simply that he supported Mendes France or that he stayed with de Gaulle when the miasma of disenchantment caused others to fall by the side. It is the insistence with which Mauriac puts politically induced actions—such as the torture of Algerians—in a moral context so that a *moral* judgment is inescapable. And those who have crossed swords with him in recent years have a right to say "Who would have thought the old man had so much blood in him?" For Mauriac has not always been kind or gentle. Not even his return to the pages of the more conservative *Figaro* will calm the passions he has stirred in others.

What I Believe does not alter the features of the Mauriac the years have revealed to us. At most it etches some lines more deeply. What could be more Mauriacean than the last section, labelled "Repentance," which begins: "I refuse to delete anything from this book, but on re-reading it, I feel scruples on two points." For if one were to construct from all that he has written a book of quotations, *Pensées* of Mauriac, it inevitably would have certain characteristics.

There would be an almost unvarying unity and consistency of tone. For Mauriac is one of those "who, even in childhood, realize that they are moving towards an unknown sea. At the very beginning of their journey they are amazed by the bitter violence of the wind and taste the salt upon their lips. On they go until at last, when the final dune has been surmounted, they find themselves in a world of spume and blown sand which seems to speak to them of a passion that is infinite." Mauriac is right to say that the man he is can be found in the child he was. And his intense concern has found remarkably similar expression in whatever literary form he chose. Is there not the same tone in these two quotations, the first from a novel, *Lines of Life* (*Destins*):

He found a heady delight in his certainty that he was the lowest of the low, but rejoiced, too, that this knowledge, by itself, made for his spiritual advancement. To those who live in God everything has its uses.

and this from *What I Believe*:

Lord, am I not finding satisfaction even in this avowal [of my hedonism]? Am I not looking for pleasure under Your gaze as I try to cleanse myself? Am I not a simulator at this very moment as I write these lines?

And could one confidently assign to either book the statement that "We possess forever the creature we have given up."?

The *Pensées* of Mauriac would be the work of a moralist, a designation he disclaims. But for Mauriac, "everything is serious, everything involves eternity"; and "the marks left by one individual on another are eternal." Although we may be imprisoned by the trivial, life itself is not trivial. Each action, each thought is subject to examination and judgment.

These *Pensées* would be, further, the work of a Christian moralist. "We love Someone who said 'Blessed are the pure in heart. . . .' Someone who said to pluck out our eye if our eye offend us." "Who would have imagined that two pieces of wood placed one upon the other could assume as many shapes as there are individual destinies."

And, finally, these *Pensées,* which would return again and again to the same themes, would resist all neat systematizing, they would leave unresolved the contradictions and tensions which are the very source and substance of Mauriac's fierce passion, a passion which remains to this day almost undiminished.

These surely are the elements of Mauriac's greatness, the reasons that he has been able to touch some readers to the quick, so that they respond to him with the immediacy of an exposed nerve. He has written that "I want to leave an account of my personal vision behind me. . . . I want to reach and touch as many people as possible. But touching means wounding. Books are violent things — violations sometimes — and they pierce some hearts deeply."

Can it be questioned that he has made his personal vision as indelible as the words of man will allow? That among his many novels there are at least four or five that will outlast the strictures of Maritain, the jibes of Gide and the slashing attacks of Sartre? For with all his faults about him, for all his parochialism, his narrowness of vision, his occasionally pinched style, his involutions of thought and feeling, he has established a Mauriacean country that is as firmly fixed as Dickens' London, as Faulkner's Yoknapatawpha County, as the provinces of Chekhov.

Whatever happens to Bordeaux, to les Landes, to the family estate of Malagar, there will always be in his novels a country where a pitiless sun beats down; where time is held in abeyance and a sluggish torpor is laid on the earth; where a strange supernatural beast crouches in a cloudy sky, waiting to be motivated by some force of unknown origin; where, on the dry cracked ground, whose heat mingles with that of living bodies, hands reach out and faces turn toward each other. It is a country in which evil is not dissolved in analyses of heredity or society, class or psyche, but where indeed these very factors contribute to make that evil palpable and palpitating. It is a country in which every action leaves its mark on the person both in this world and another.

It is the permanence of this country and the penetration of this vision, which allow those to whom these books speak directly to refer to their creator, with admiration, gratitude and confidence, as the great Mauriac.

Francois Mauriac

THE FINAL ANSWER

If I were to give a human reason for my fidelity to Christ in this evening of my life, I would call it His quieting of the radical anguish that is in me. This anguish is not to be confused with the fear spoken of by Lucretius, that gives birth to gods. For anguish is not fear. My very singular anguish, which I did not learn from anyone, tormented me from the moment I began to grow aware of the tragedy implied in the fact of being a man; that is to say, a creature condemned to death and who lives under a stay of execution for an unknown length of time. This stay grows shorter each year and my life resembles that "sorrowful flesh" which one of Balzac's heroes contemplated with horror as it shrank to the size of a coin in his trembling hand.

Anguish is so consubstantial to the human condition that is already cruelly manifest in childhood. I still remember, to the point of reliving them, those early torments in my unlighted bedroom; I still hear those slow and heavy footsteps on the stairway; and I still bury my head beneath the blankets. I still feel the hot tears that coursed down my cheeks when, as a boarding-school student, I watched the flickering gas flame trace vacillating shadows on the walls of the dormitory. Perhaps I was a small, timid boy who felt himself less robust than the others in the playground filled with noise and quarrels.

From THE SON OF MAN, by Francois Mauriac (World Publishing Co., Cleveland, 1960). Reprinted by permission of the author and the publisher.

Perhaps I was afraid of being called to the head of the room by a contemptuous teacher who was quite capable of making me appear ridiculous and idiotic before my classmates. Perhaps, too, I remember the room in my parents' home where someone had died some time before and where the shutters remained forever closed upon a horrible mystery. Each object in it seemed to have suffered death's somber magic: the glass of water, the arrested pendulum, the armchair still sagging near the fireplace where the fire would never again be lighted.

Yes, for many children anguish is a secret and permanent state. To keep from going insane, I needed the limitless love which my mother poured out on me, the touch of her hand upon my brow during those terrible nights, the comfort of her breath in my hair, and the sound of her voice softly complaining: "What's the matter, silly child? What are you afraid of? I am here; close your eyes and go to sleep."

What, indeed, was tormenting me? My memories help me acknowledge this fact: anguish does not come from without; it is in no way linked to the catastrophes of a given age. The anguished child that I was lived in a time when the war we were fighting concerned only King Behanzin and when the refrain which a blind man chanted in the courtyard of our home reminded me that the French flag had just been raised at Madagascar. There was much argument about us apropos of a certain Dreyfus but his misfortunes did not sadden me at all. In fact, almost all the famous people (people who would not have harmed a fly) had only one fear: that Dreyfus would not be convicted again.

My anguish of later years already existed in that child of a comfortable family in the third Republic—bourgeois, powerful, rich, peaceful, although capable of aggression for a good cause.

Of course, I do not pretend that the era of calamities which began in 1914 (the first premonitions of which were evident much earlier) has not nourished the anguish of modern man or that there was no causal relationship between the unhappiness of the times and the existential anguish of "being in the world." But these events, however tragic they were, did not create my anguish, even though they obliged me to relate it to the vissicitudes of history. Let us say that we can no longer "distract" ourselves from them, in accordance with Pascal's use of that word. I believe that even in those ages when history confronted human nature with nothing that was singularly tragic, in the peaceful and happy ages—peaceful and happy at least for the privileged classes, because there is never a happy age for the working class—man was smitten by the unhappiness that comes of being a man who loves and is not loved; who is loved and does not love; who had a son and lost him; who was young and is so no longer; who was strong and healthy and who one day heard a doctor tell him, after a long examination, "We might try an operation . . . ," and who hears the automobiles in the streets, a radio playing upstairs, a woman's laughter, but who knows that in six months he will be dead. But even if this trial is spared him there remains the adequate torture (as Michelet called old age) of the gradual deterioration of strength, the decline of the mind, the slow and noiseless approach of ineluctable dissolution.

In this matter I disagree with Michelet and so many others and I exclaim with Lacordaire: "Gentlemen, I bring you happiness." I bring you the kind of happiness that a Christian begins to discover at my age. In the measure that I have grown old, anguish has loosened its grip on me. "The man who grows old becomes more aware of the eternal," says Romano Guardini. "He is less agitated and the voices from beyond are better heard. The encroachment of eternity pales the reality of time."

There is a prayer by Saint Gertrude, who must have been very old when she uttered it, in which she calls Christ "the love of the evening of my life" and in which she says: "O my Jesus of life's evening, let me fall asleep in you quietly. . . ." But all of this was already expressed at the dawn of the Christian Era when the aged Simeon pressed the infant God to his breast: *Nunc dimittis servum tuum, Domine*. . . .

Christ is not a defense which I have erected against anguish; on the contrary, anguish was a permanent state during the days of my stormy youth when I did not have recourse to Him, when I dwelt apart from Him. No, my anguish did not create God. The quieting I now experience, the silence that falls upon my last days, permits me finally to be attentive to the answer which was unceasingly given during my tormented life, but to which I preferred my suffering because I preferred my sin. What more do I know today than I did as a despairing adolescent? The adolescent loves neither happiness nor peace. It took me a long time to learn to love God. I can say nothing on this subject that is not part of my life: as an adolescent I loved my anguish and I preferred it to God. Far from inciting me to imagine a God to deliver me, my anguish provided me with reasons and excuses to escape the presence, in me and about me, of a love to which I preferred an unhappiness born of covetousness.

It is not anguish which creates the Father in heaven whom Christ taught us to know and to love. It was rather my anguish, the somber delectation that lasted throughout my interminable youth—I say interminable because my heart remains young even though I am not—it was this delectation in anguish that inclined me to turn away from God and even deny that He existed. It furnished me with arguments and proofs against His goodness, against His love.

This is undoubtedly not true of all men. But it is true of those writers and poets who cherish in their anguish the very source of their inspiration, and more precisely in that form of anguish which is born of an attraction for a God who is rejected by flesh and blood. I have often applied to myself the image from Maurice de Guérin in which he compared his thought to a heavenly fire that burns on a horizon between two worlds. It is the torture of being incapable of chosing between the world and God that constitutes in effect the drama of many artists—a drama which both torments and delights them.

"If thou didst know the gift of God," Christ said to the Samaritan woman. And what is the gift of God? It is precisely the opposite of anguish. "Peace I leave with you; my peace I give to you," Christ repeated to His friends on the last night, before He entered into His agony. It is precisely this peace which we do not want; it appears redoutable to us because we do not love peace. "Arise, desired tempests!" was the cry of René at the dawn of the Romantic Age; and this cry reveals the vocation of so many young people to unhappiness. I went first of all to the damned poets and they attracted me to the prince of darkness and his eternal unhappiness. Was this literature? Yes, but it was a strange literature in which despair was so often, in surrealist circles, authenticated by suicide. Saint John denounces this hatred of peace; he tells us that light came into the world and that men refused it because they preferred darkness. The creature seeks darkness to obliterate himself. The victory of Christ in a life is summed up in this difficult acceptance of peace in light.

I am aware of this objection: Christianity itself is anguish. But it is not enough to say that there is a Christian anguish. All those who revolted against Christianity in the nineteenth century accused it of being against nature, of having darkened the world, of having calumniated life. It is true that the name of Christianity masks many contradictory tendencies which set Christians at odds with one another. Those who are called to love one another have burned each other. There are many mansions in the Father's house. And one of them, from Saint Augustine through Calvin and Jansen, was erected under the sign of fear and trembling: anguish in the strictest sense of the word. But there is another anguish which is less harsh: that of love which is totally contained in the regret of having offended the loved one, in the fear of no longer being loved by him, and of no longer feeling ourselves capable of loving him. The love of the creature for the Creator is no more exempt from what Marcel Proust calls the intermittences of the heart than human love. But this is not the anguish we refer to when we speak of fear and trembling.

Monsieur de Saint-Cyran has always seemed to me to be the worst kind of theologian. Let us say that in France, to speak only of France, Port-Royal is still the most illustrious source of that anguish which is centered upon an obsession with personal salvation. The Infinite Being refuses or gives His grace according to an unpredictable plan to a creature tainted from birth, totally impotent except to do evil (for in what concerns evil, human nature has the power of a god). We are delivered naked, trembling, disarmed, to an arbitrary God. This is the root of Jansenist anguish.

It is impossible to indicate in a few words the contents of the immense work in which, over the centuries, a whole school of Christian thinkers have collaborated. I will simply allude to the permanent source of anguish and even of despair that a certain theology has premised upon a wounded heart. It has generated innumerable and lamentable progeny, the terror of Catholic confessors: those scrupulous souls obsessed by trifles, adorers of a niggling divinity with whom we must bargain craftily. Andre Gide denounced Catholics for their "cramp of salvation." This cramp is so painful that many young people who began by following Christ drew away from Him to escape the frightful obligation of rendering an account of their least desire, their least thought. They threw the whole Christian heritage overboard. "What is wonderful about Communism," a recent convert to Marxism told me one day, "is that my personal salvation no longer interests me."

What I propose as a defense against this form of anguish is another anguish which is generative of peace and joy. I propose a kind of spiritual homeopathy, that is, a release from anguish through anguish. Obsession with our personal salvation will not be dominated and conquered in us unless it is transposed to the order of charity. It goes without saying that we should nourish the hope of salvation and that the whole of a Christian life ought to tend toward eternal life. But if it is clear that we ought to have a passionate desire for salvation, we should not be obsessed with it in the pathological sense of the word. In my youth I was frequently seduced by the words which Pascal put in Christ's mouth: "I thought of you in my agony. I lost so much blood for you." These words impress me less today because I discern in such a desire for redemptive blood the complacency of a creature resigned to the eternal damnation of most of the human race, and not agonized by the thought that he is set apart with a small flock of the elect.

Anguish transmuted into charity, *anguish for another,* delivers us from the terror felt by so many Christian souls before the mystery of predestination and liberates us from an obsession with personal salvation, not in respect to what is essential but in respect to what is morbid. Our anguish then becomes more than a matter of personal concern: it embraces mankind or, at least, that part of mankind which is "the neighbor" for us and can extend to a social class or to entire peoples. For a worker priest, the neighbor is the whole working class, as the Jews were for us during the Nazi persecution.

For Sartre "hell is other people"; but for us, others are Christ. He tells us Himself that the Son of Man is come to save what is lost, *all* that is lost and not merely this one or that one for whom He would have consecrated a special, miserly drop of His blood.

The Christian life is first of all a personal relationship between each one of us and God. "You have not chosen me; I have chosen you." It goes without saying that the extension of our anguish to embrace the suffering of men will not yield all of its fruits unless our apostolate is rooted in a life of close intimacy with Christ. I believe, I have always believed, that the Christian life is essentially a friendship, a love (and therefore that which is most personal, most individual), that each one of us has been called by his name, and that at the beginning of every conversion there is this encounter at the turning of the road spoken of by Lacordaire—an encounter with an adorable being, demanding, tenacious, whom nothing discourages, and to whom we prefer so many creatures whom we shortly forsake or who forsake us. But He is always there, never so close to us as when we believe Him to be absent, awaiting His hour which, in the case of many men, is unfortunately the last, when there is no longer any possibility of betrayal.

But what is the reality of this Christ whom all believers strive to imitate, unless it be that He took upon Himself our human anguish? Therefore, we must also take upon ourselves the anguish of each other. The saints did so literally, to the point of identifying themselves with the Father's abandonment of His Son in the horror of the night. This secret of Christ's agony was profoundly understood by Bernanos. And this is what gives his fictional priests, particularly the country priest, their mysterious density. For us, as simple faithful, it is sufficient to unite ourselves with the anguish, experienced by Christ, in our brothers.

Here, then, is the strange remedy for anguish which I propose: peace and joy are the fruits of anguish. "Peace I leave with you, my peace I give to you: not as the world gives do I give to you." We understand now the profound meaning of the last promise which the Son of Man made to us before entering into His agony: peace and joy in this plentitude of suffering which consists in espousing, each one according to his vocation, the suffering of the hungry, the persecuted, the imprisoned, the tortured, the exploited. This is the Christian paradox.

We know that there is a difference between human hope and spiritual hope. We may lose all hope for the temporal salvation of mankind and still await the kingdom of God. In the very midst of the Atomic Age, we await it confidently. But it must not be concluded from this that our hope concerns only eternity; it also concerns the dark world of the living. For the crimes of the will to power which sum up temporal history do not prevent the leaven of which Christ speaks from working tirelessly in the human mass. The fire which He came to cast upon the earth is always smoldering and the bloodiest years of history are nevertheless years of grace.

"Thy kingdom come," we pray in the Our Father. Millions and millions of human beings have prayed thus over the nearly two thousand years since this prayer was taught to us, and with the absolute certitude of being answered. Indeed the prayer is already answered; the kingdom has already come; it is among us, within us in such a way that we are never defeated except in appearance. And as our anguish is the very condition of our peace, our defeat is the very condition of our victory. "Fear not; I have overcome the world." He who challenged the world so boldly did so at the very hour when He was about to be betrayed, outraged, made a laughingstock, nailed to the gibbet of a slave.

Saint Paul tells us that all of creation groans and suffers the pains of childbirth. Our anguish is indeed inspired by childbirth and it seems interminable by our ephemeral standards. But those of us who have kept the faith know what the end will be. To those who succumb to anguish and who are about to lose heart, we can do no better than repeat what Saint Paul affirmed to the faithful of Rome: "Who shall separate us from the love of Christ? Shall tribulation, or distress, or persecution, or hunger, or nakedness, or danger, or the sword? But in all these things we overcome because of him who has loved us."

BIBLIOGRAPHY

Cormeau, Nelly, *L'art de François Mauriac*. Paris: Grosset, 1951.

Dillistone, F. W., *The Novelist and the Passion Story*. New York: Sheed and Ward, 1960.

Du Bos, Charles, *François Mauriac et le problème du romancier catholique*. Paris: Corrêa, 1933.

Fowlie, Wallace, *Clowns and Angels*: *Studies in Modern French Literature*. New York: Sheed and Ward, 1943.

Greene, Graham, *The Lost Childhood and Other Essays*. London: Eyre & Spottiswoode, 1951.

Heppenstall, Rayner, *The Double Image*: *Mutations of Christian Mythology in the Work of Four French Catholic Writers of Today and Yesterday*. London: Secker & Warburg, 1947.

Hourdin, Georges, *Mauriac, romancier chrétien*. Paris: Éditions du Temps présent, 1945.

Jaloux, Edmond, *François Mauriac romancier, Préface à Le romancier et ses personages*. Paris: Corrêa, 1933.

Jarrett-Kerr, *François Mauriac*. New Haven: Yale, 1954.

Madeleine, Sister, *The role of the unconscious in the novels of Mauriac*. Fordham University Ph.D. dissertation (unpublished), 1949.

Majault, Joseph, *Mauriac et l'art du roman*. Paris: R. Laffont, 1946.

Maloney, Michael F., *François Mauriac*: *A Critical Study*. Denver: Alan Swallow, 1958.

North, Robert J., *Le catholicisme dans l'oeuvre de François Mauriac*. Paris: Editions du Conquistador, 1950.

O'Donnell, Donat, *Maria Cross*: *Imaginative Patterns in a Group of Modern Catholic Writers*. New York: Oxford University Press, 1952.

Pell, Elsie, *François Mauriac in Search of the Infinite*. New York: Philosophical Library, 1947.

Periodicals

Fowlie, Wallace, "Francois Mauriac," *Kenyon Review,* 5 (Spring 1943), 189-200.

Rubin, Louis D., Jr., "Francois Mauriac and the Freedom of the Religious Novelist," *The Southern Review,* 2, (Winter 1966), 17-39.

Vial, Fernand, "Francois Mauriac Criticism, A Bibliographical Study," *Thought,* 27, (Summer 1952), 235-260.

Vial, Fernand, "Mauriac and Recent Critics," *Renascence,* 8, (Winter 1955), 88-94.

CONTRIBUTORS

Sister Anita Caspary

(FORMERLY KNOWN AS MOTHER MARY HUMILIATA, I.H.M.)

b. 1915; B.A., I.H.C.; M.A., U.S.C.; Ph.D., Stanford U.; President, Immaculate Heart College 1957-1963; Superior General 1963-; contributor to *PMLA; Huntington Library Quarterly; Twentieth Century Literature; College English.*

Francois Mauriac

b. 1885; studied at University of Bordeaux; novelist; playwright; critic; newspaper writer; Member of French Academy and winner of Nobel Prize for Literature in 1952. Among his writings are *Le baisèr au lépreux* (1922); *Genetrix* (1923); *Le Désert de l'amour* (1925); *Le Noeud de Vipères* (1932); *Vie de Jesus* (1936); and several volumes of collected articles titled *Journal.*

Henri Peyre (Maurice)

b. 1901; studied at the Sorbonne and Ecole Normale Superieure; B.A., 1918; Licence, 1922; Agregation, 1924; Doctorat, 1932. Yale University Sterling Professor of French, 1938-. Visiting Professorships University of Lyons, University of Chicago, Cornell University, Columbia University; editor of *Essays in Honor of Albert Feuillert,* 1943, *Pensees de Baudelaire: recueillies et classes* 1951, *Baudelaire, a Collection of Critical Essays* 1962, author of *Writers and Their Critics: A Study of Misun-*

derstanding 1944, *Les generations litteraires* 1948, *The Cultural Migration* 1953, *The Contemporary French Novel* 1955, *Observations on Life, Literature and Learning in America* 1961, *Literature and Sincerity* 1963; contributor to numerous professional journals and commentator for "Splendors of Christendom" series in *Time* and *Life*.

Michael F. Moloney

b. 1903 - d. 1961; B.A., University of Notre Dame 1926; M.A., Georgetown University 1931; Ph.D., University of Illinois 1939. Teaching positions at St. Viator College 1933-38, University of Illinois 1938-39, Marquette University 1944-1961; author of *John Donne* 1944, "Christian Humanism: Past History and Current Relevance," *Spiritual Life,* 1958.

Neville Braybrooke

b. 1923; British; military service 1941-46; clown in a touring circus 1946-53; editor of *T. S. Eliot*: *A Symposium for His 75th Birthday* 1958, *The Wind and the Rain*: *An Easter Book* 1962, *Teilhard de Chardin*: *A Symposium* 1964; author of several articles on London and contributor to the *Guardian, Observer, London Times, Saturday Review,* and *New York Herald Tribune.*

James Finn

b. 1924; attended Purdue University 1942-43, 1945-46; M.A., University of Chicago 1949; military service 1943-45; teaching positions at University of Nebraska 1949-50, N.Y.U. 1950-51, University of Chicago 1953-55; assoc. editor of *Commonweal* 1955-61; editor of *Worldview* 1961-; director of publications for the Council on Religion and World Affairs; author of *Sabres of France* 1961, *Protest*: *Pacifism and Politics* 1968.